Drive and Stroll

Hertfordshire

Liz Moynihan

COUNTRYSIDE BOOKS
NEWBURY BERKSHIRE

First published 2006
© Liz Moynihan 2006

COUNTRYSIDE BOOKS
3 Catherine Road
Newbury, Berkshire

To view our complete range of books,
please visit us at
www.countrysidebooks.co.uk

ISBN 1 85306 973 6
EAN 978 1 85306 973 4

To Beetle, my third walking companion

Cover picture of Westmill, supplied by Derek Forss

Photographs by the author
Designed by Peter Davies, Nautilus Design

Produced through MRM Associates Ltd., Reading
Typeset by Jean Cussons Typesetting, Diss, Norfolk
Printed by Borcombe Printers, Romsey

Contents

AREA MAP SHOWING THE LOCATIONS OF THE WALKS

N

Hertfordshire

Hitchin

Bishop's
Stortford

St.
Albans

Hemel
Hempstead

Watford

Contents

PUBLISHER'S NOTE

We hope that you obtain considerable enjoyment from this book; great care has been taken in its preparation. Although at the time of publication all routes followed public rights of way or permitted paths, diversion orders can be made and permissions withdrawn.

We cannot, of course, be held responsible for such diversion orders and any inaccuracies in the text which result from these or any other changes to the routes nor any damage which might result from walkers trespassing on private property. We are anxious though that all details covering the walks are kept up to date and would therefore welcome information from readers which would be relevant to future editions.

The simple sketch maps that accompany the walks in this book are based on notes made by the author whilst checking the routes on the ground. However, for the benefit of a proper map, we do recommend that you purchase the relevant Ordnance Survey sheet covering your walk. The Ordnance Survey maps are widely available, especially through booksellers and local newsagents.

Introduction

Hertfordshire has an astonishing variety of historic landscapes. There are remnants of old hunting forest and tiny lanes that lead off the beaten track through wonderful countryside to pretty villages and hamlets. The scenery varies from wide, rolling plains to deep, wooded valleys or the hilly outcrops of the Chilterns. One advantage of the county's proximity to London is the array of historic mansions, with their attendant parks and estates. Many of these 'country seats' were built for London entrepreneurs and noble families, while, in the gracious towns and large villages, beautiful old houses proclaim the wealth of local merchants and landowners. A rich tapestry indeed!

All the walks in this book start where it is possible to park with relative ease, and they range in length from 2 to 6 miles. They are very varied and have a historical and/or wildlife flavour, often exploring the relationship of the man-made environment with the surrounding countryside. Several long distance routes – the Icknield Way, the Hertfordshire Way, and the Chiltern Way – traverse the county, and some walks take in sections of these tracks. This book aims to make the walks easy to follow, but please be aware of how much conditions change from season to season: for instance, many signposts can be hidden by dense vegetation in summer; conditions underfoot can change drastically; and different views open up when the trees are bare.

Part of the fun of an invigorating walk is looking forward to a drink and meal in a good pub or café, and suggestions for suitable refreshment stops are included with every walk. It is possible to park in pub car parks, but do please confirm with the landlord that it is all right for you to leave your car in his car park while you do the walk. It is also important to telephone first if you are bringing a group. Please use common sense wherever you park, and do not park across entrances or private parking places.

Finally, your walk will be much more enjoyable if you are properly dressed and equipped. Long trousers and long sleeves will protect against overgrown vegetation, especially in high summer; boots are useful if paths become rutted; and a hat is vital when the days get hot and sunny. And, remember the Country Code and shut gates, keep dogs on leads, and leave nothing but your footprints.

So, drive, park, stroll and enjoy!

Liz Moynihan

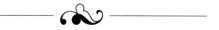

1 | Ayot St Lawrence

George Bernard Shaw's residence at the Old Rectory is now in the care of the National Trust

Distance 5 miles   **Terrain** Undulating
Map OS Explorer 182 St Albans and Hatfield (GR 695733)

How to get there

Ayot St Lawrence is signposted north from the B653 road near Wheathampstead. **Parking:** Near the Brocket Arms pub in the main street, or outside St Lawrence's church if there is no service.

Drive and Stroll

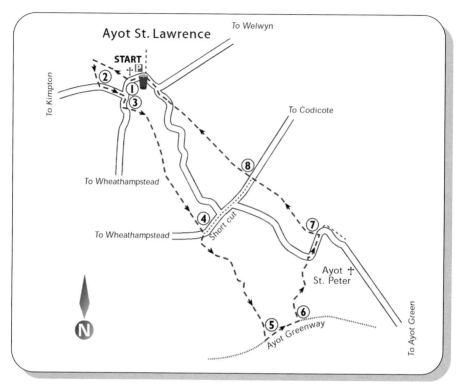

Introduction

Beautiful all year round, but especially in early May when the woods have a carpet of bluebells and the lanes are fringed with cow parsley, this walk explores the rolling farmland and woodland between Ayot St Lawrence, with its 15th and 16th century dwellings and the hamlet of Ayot St Peter. Ayot St Lawrence has royal connections which go back to Edward the Confessor and William the Conqueror. Still visible is the manor house where Henry VIII courted Catherine, the daughter of its owner, Sir Richard Parr. The walk explores the village's two churches and then sets out through tranquil farmland and woods – one a nature reserve containing traditional coppiced hornbeam – and then proceeds along a section of the Ayot Greenway towards Ayot St Peter with its manor house and Victorian church.

Refreshments

The Brocket Arms is named after a lord of the manor. This is an attractive half-timbered pub dating back to Tudor times and has a wonderful inglenook fireplace. It is open all day every day, and serves excellent beers and food (game a speciality). It also has accommodation. Telephone: 01438 820250.

THE WALK

Turn left out of the pub and walk along the main street, passing the ruined church on the right with the white Georgian rectory opposite.

In 1775, the lord of the manor, Sir Lyonel Lyde, began to demolish the 12th century church of St Lawrence in the main street because it spoilt the view from his newly-built Ayot House. When an injunction was issued to stop him, the church was left as a ruin, and Sir Lyonel built a new church, designed by Nicholas Revett in the classical style.

To view the church, just past a white cottage, take a signed footpath to the right through two kissing gates and go over the meadows to the church. Go through another kissing gate to the right of the building, and then bear left behind it, along a wide track to the road.

Turn left along the road, passing **Shaw's Corner** on the right.

George Bernard Shaw came to live in Ayot at the Edwardian red brick New Rectory. The story goes that he was impressed by a tombstone in the churchyard inscribed 'Mary

Anne South, born 1825, died 1895. Her time was short'! His house (now National Trust) is just as he left it when he died at the age of 94.

At a road junction, turn right downhill, ignoring a footpath to the right at the end of the Shaw's garden. Bear left round the corner, and then left off the road onto a bridleway signed to **Codicote Road** and **Ayot Greenway**.

The bridleway goes for some distance along the edge of fields and woodlands, and then opens into a large field on the right. Keep ahead and soon bear left into woodland. This is a permissive route running parallel to the bridleway through **Stocking Springs Wood** (a Herts and Middlesex Wildlife Trust Nature Reserve and an example of coppiced hornbeam trees which encourages a wonderful array of wildflowers). A kissing gate at the end of the path gives onto the main track and thence the **Codicote** road.

(Turn left for a SHORT CUT.)

For the main walk, cross the road slightly to the left and follow the bridleway (signed to **Hunter's Bridge** and **Waterend Lane**) along a well-defined route alongside woodland.

The path bears slightly to the left and then goes into a field. Go through a gateway and continue ahead along the edge of woodland. The bridleway continues round the woodland, and then goes left past some conifers (signed). Keeping the conifers on the left, continue down a small hill; then follow the woodland round, keeping it on the left. Bear left through a gap in the hedge (signed) and then bear right, keeping the hedge on the right at the edge of an arable field.

Just before an old brick railway bridge (**Hunter's Bridge**), which carried the branch line from Welwyn Garden City to Luton (closed 1960), turn right and climb onto the old railway track, now **Ayot Greenway.** Walk along it to the left.

When the land on the left rises, look for a footpath to the left (arrow on tree). Go over a stile and across a small field towards the grounds of 17th century Ayot Place. Bear right along the drive, alongside the garden. Ignore a footpath to the right and continue along the drive to a junction. Turn right here (signed)

and continue to ornate gates. Go through a door in the right-hand pillar and leave via another door onto a lane. Go along the lane, passing an overgrown graveyard on the right. Turn right if you want to view St Peter's church of 1875.

To continue the main walk, take the signposted bridleway to the left by **Tamarisk Cottage**. Continue past a dell, ignoring a footpath to the right and going gently downhill to reach the **Codicote** road.

Cross the road and continue uphill (signed). At a crossing of farm tracks keep ahead towards the houses of **Ayot St Lawrence**. Go through a hedge onto a lane and bear right, passing immaculate, converted properties. Continue, bearing left at a road junction along the thickly wooded lane leading back to the **Brocket Arms**.

For a diversion to glimpse **Ayot House** and the **Manor House** of the Parrs, before reaching the pub, turn right through a gateway and walk along a bridleway signed to these properties.

Place of Interest Nearby

The Jacobean **Hatfield House**, about 8 miles to the south of Ayot St Lawrence, is the seat of the Marquess of Salisbury; it has exquisite gardens. Telephone: 01707 287010.

2 | Frithsden, Nettleden and Great Gaddesden

The church of St John the Baptist, Great Gaddesden

Distance 6 miles **Terrain** Hilly
Map OS Explorer 182 St Albans and Hatfield (GR 005093)

How to get there

Take the A4146 Leighton Buzzard to Hemel Hempstead road. **Parking**: Between Berkhamsted and Frithsden, follow signs to the castle and church (along Castle Street) off the High Street. At a road junction, go left, and then right before the station, going under the railway into Brownlow Road. Go over a crossroads and bear right round the castle to a T-junction. Turn left here along New Road to reach another T-junction near Berkhamsted Golf Club. The car park is on the left, with a war memorial over the road. Parking is difficult in the narrow lanes of the villages.

Drive and Stroll

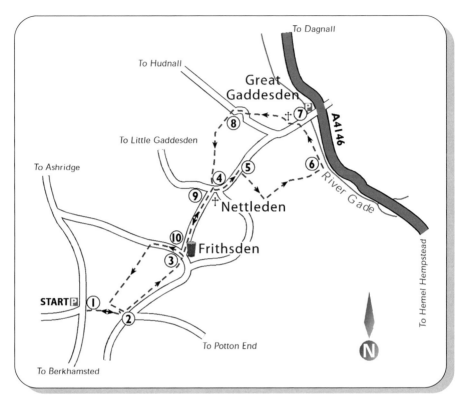

Introduction

This is one of the hilliest walks in Hertfordshire, dipping down into three wooded valleys of the Chilterns to visit three tiny but fascinating villages. This area, near the river Gade, is full of wildlife and historical interest. The walk goes downhill to Frithsden, on the edge of lovely National Trust woodland. From here a spooky Roman road reaches a summit which offers great views of Ashridge House on one side and Gaddesden Place on the other. The track then descends into a cutting to reach Nettleden with its attractive old cottages. Another summit is reached in old woodland before the route drops to the water meadows at Great Gaddesden. Here public access has been granted through to Water End, where there are vestiges of an old water garden, a picturesque feature in the former grounds of Gaddesden Place. From Great Gaddesden with its 12th century church and early 17th century cottages, the walk climbs through fields to a Buddhist temple in the hamlet of St Margaret's, once the site of an ancient nunnery, before returning through fields and woods to the parking place.

Refreshments

The Alford Arms is a delightful pub in Frithsden, which once brewed its own beer. It is named after Lady Alford, a previous custodian of nearby Ashridge. As well as an imaginative range of main dishes, the menu also offers delicious 'Small Plates', which are perfect for a lunch break. Telephone: 01442 864480.

THE WALK

From the car park, cross the road to the war memorial and walk down the signed bridleway to the right of it. Continue ahead across the golf course into sections of trees, avoiding all subsidiary tracks and eventually walking downhill.

The bridleway reaches a road at a signpost. Almost going back on yourself, turn along another signed bridleway for a short distance and take the first path to the right at a marker post. This path crosses a shallow ditch, goes through wooden barriers, and follows a narrow path ahead through hedges bordering gardens to come out onto a road through wooden barriers (arrow-marked). Cross the road to a metal signpost and continue ahead along a now broad track. Ignore a footpath to the right and continue along the main track going gently downhill through the beautiful brackeny woodland of **Little Frithsden Copse**. Steps help on a steep section just before the track reaches a lane by the **Alford Arms** pub in the pretty hamlet of **Frithsden**.

Cross and continue down the lane ahead alongside the pub. Ignore the lane to the left by an attractive pargetted cottage and continue uphill passing the gates to Frithsden Vineyard (sadly no longer producing wine). This Roman road, justly named **Spooky Lane**, turns into a much rougher track which continues uphill.

*At the top there are good views, with distant glimpses over on the left of **Ashridge House** and, on the right ahead, of **Gaddesden Place**.*

Ignore all other paths and go downhill, walking under the arch of a bridge which once took a driveway into Ashridge, to come out into the hamlet of Nettleden. Continue ahead to the road.

Turn right along the road for a short distance. Then, opposite the **church of St Lawrence** , turn left up leafy **Piper's Hill** passing **Neo-Gothic Nettleden House**.

5

Before the top of the hill look for a public footpath signpost on the right pointing to **Potten End**. Turn right here, walking along the edge of a field, with a hedge on the left and good views down into the valley. Carry on ahead into **High Park Wood**. The track forks and this walk bears left through the wood. Ignore a path to the left (marker post) and go round a pit to the right. Then go left again to continue just inside the edge of the wood. Ignore a path to the right near the end of the wood and continue straight on, leaving the wood to walk through fields down into the valley of the **river Gade**, with **Gaddesden Place** on the hillside ahead. Go through a metal kissing gate into **watermeadows** and continue ahead.

6

At a wire fence, go left through a metal gate into Open Access meadows. Further along the river to the right near **Water End** was a **Domesday cornmill** and old watercress beds can still be seen. Walk to the left along a fence then continue on through the bumpy water meadows in the general direction of Great Gaddesden church. Cross a stile at a footpath signpost onto a lane into the village. **Wyevale Garden Centre** (parking) is to the right.

7

Go slightly right and then left along

Church Meadow, bearing left past pretty cottages and the school to go through the lychgate into the churchyard.

*The fine **church of St John the Baptist** has an Early English chancel. Outside there are five altar tombs in a row, and a 15th century tower with curious gargoyles. Two huge lumps of Hertfordshire pudding stone grace the churchyard.*

Go up the left-hand edge of the churchyard to find a hidden stile at the top corner. Cross the stile and walk to the right alongside the church wall to a kissing gate. Go through and walk diagonally half right across a meadow to a gap in a hedgerow. Go through a kissing gate and continue on the same line diagonally across another field. (New kissing gates were being put in when I walked.) Go through another kissing gate and walk uphill alongside woodland on the right. Come out through another kissing gate at a signpost onto a lane in the hamlet of **St Margaret's**.

8

Turn left along the road for a short way, passing the entrance gates to the **Amaravati Buddhist Monastery**. Turn right just here along a footpath signed to **Nettleden** beside a drive by **Beech Tree Cottage**. When the drive bends to the left, carry straight on along a narrow path through a strip of woodland. The path continues over a stile into a field, passing between a hedge on the left and a fence on the right and going steadily downhill past field boundaries and through a metal barrier onto a lane in the hamlet of **Nettleden**.

 9

Turn left and very shortly right to return up the lane past **Roman Farm**. Instead of retracing your steps through the embankment, climb up steps by a footpath signpost to the left of the lane and walk uphill through trees high above **Spooky Lane**. Pass some lumps of dressed stone, all that remains of the former **Ashridge drive bridge**, and continue ahead (arrow marker). Go over a stile and bear right to come out onto the lane at the junction of paths. Carry on down the **Roman road** into **Frithsden** and the **Alford Arms** pub.

 10

To finish the walk, turn right here along the little lane through the hamlet of Frithsden, passing a National Trust Ashridge sign on the left. Ignore a footpath to the right, but shortly after this take a footpath to the left, signed to **Berkhamsted Common**. Follow the main path, which ascends through beautiful woodland, ignoring all subsidiary paths. The track veers slightly right by a marker post, then continues through fencing to a roadway at a signpost. Cross the road, go through arrow-marked fencing and continue on between hedges to come out on the golf course. Turn left along the edge of the course, continuing on past a golf tee on an obvious track bearing slightly right through woodland. Avoid other paths and keep ahead to come out at the road at a metal signpost. Turn right almost back on yourself along another bridleway, which is the same one used on the outward journey. Follow the main track through the golf course back to the car park.

Places of Interest Nearby

Ashridge Estate (National Trust), which is passed on this walk, has magnificent woods, commons and downland along a ridge of the Chilterns, and the **Bridgewater Monument**. Telephone: 01442 851227. The ruins of the **Norman Berkhamsted Castle** are just over 2 miles away, and have an unusual double moat. Telephone: 01442 867842.

3 | Aldbury

The pond and stocks at Aldbury

Distance 5½ miles   **Terrain** Undulating
Map OS Explorer 181 Chiltern Hills North (GR 965125)

How to get there

From the A4251 road through Berkhamsted towards Aylesbury, turn right at Northchurch onto the B4506 (Ashridge) road. After about 2½ miles, turn left, signed to Aldbury and Tring. Follow the road for a mile as it twists down into the village. **Parking**: Near the village green outside the Greyhound pub or at the recreation ground further on, down Stocks Road. There is also parking where the Ridgeway (Grim's Dyke) joins the Icknield Way (a continuation of Stocks Road, which runs through Aldbury); from here you can join the walk at point 6.

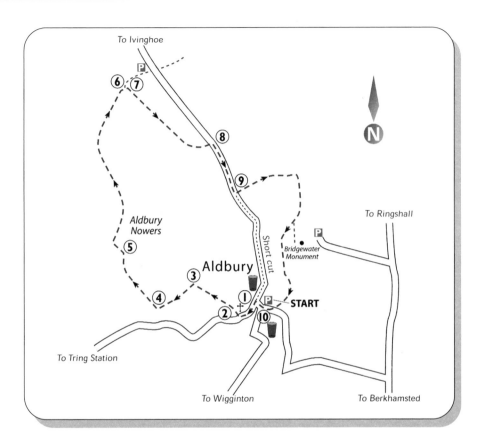

Introduction

This western part of the county, near the border with Buckinghamshire, is one of the prettiest parts of the Chilterns. Beautiful wooded Ashridge (National Trust), with its rich variety of wildlife, towers over the village of Aldbury, whose Old English name meant 'old fortified place'. The area is littered with Bronze Age tumuli radiating from Ivinghoe Beacon, just to the north, Iron Age dykes such as Grim's Ditch, which forms part of this walk, and Roman roads and remains. (It is claimed that a Roman road passed where the Valiant Trooper pub now stands.) The Grand Union canal runs through the parish, complementing the tall monument to the third Duke of Bridgewater, who built Ashridge House. He was known as 'the Canal Duke' or 'the Father of Inland Navigation', though the Grand Union canal was not built by him. The walk starts in Aldbury, where beautiful old houses and cottages cluster round a picturesque green with stocks and a whipping post

Drive and Stroll

by a large pond. The cosy village contrasts with the woods and open downland on the rest of the walk, parts of which are along the Hertfordshire Way, the Grand Union Canal Circular Walk, the Ridgeway, and the Icknield Way. The area is much used by walkers and is consequently well way-marked and signed.

Refreshments

The Greyhound, on the village green in Aldbury, offers accommodation as well as good pub meals and excellent beers. Telephone: 01442 851228. Over the road is the **Tower Farm Tea Rooms**. Telephone: 01442 851239.

THE WALK

Come out of the **Greyhound** and turn right, walking past the **Old Manor House**, with the village pond and the stocks over the road. Bear right into **Station Road**, passing the school and then the **church of St John the Baptist**.

Inside the church is a lovely 15th century brass to Sir Ralph Verney and his wife. The Pendley chapel, which is separated from the rest of the church by a fine stone screen brought from Ashridge in 1575, houses the tomb of Robert Whittingham (died 1452), whose feet rest on 'The Wild Man', while his wife has her feet on a hart.

Just beyond the church and burial ground is a public footpath signpost to **Pitstone Hill** and the **Ridgeway**.

Turn right here through a kissing gate, cross a meadow, and go over an arrow-marked stile near old farm buildings. (In the distance on the right is a view of the **Bridgewater Monument**, poking its head over the trees of the **Ashridge estate**.) Leave the meadow through an arrow-marked kissing gate on the left, and walk in the same direction as before along a narrow path by farm buildings. The route goes through a metal kissing gate, over a farm track to another kissing gate, and then along a fenced-off path. Go through another kissing gate to a junction of paths with a black wooden signpost.

Turn left here towards the **Ridgeway** to another signpost and continue straight on between fields to a metal gate. Continue on through a fenced gap down steps to another signpost at a crossroad of paths.

Turn right here up a good stony path between hedges and trees, going on for some distance to yet another signpost at a junction of tracks. Bear right here, passing a Ridgeway National Trail sign and going slightly uphill through a wooden barrier. On the left is the flower-rich chalk grassland of **Duchie's Piece Nature Reserve**. Ahead, a National Trust sign announces **Aldbury Nowers**. Walk through a more open area and then uphill into woodland and on to another signpost.

 5

Turn left here up steps; ignoring a footpath on the left, continue on up more steps. At a wooden post fork left. (There are good views over the nature reserve down into the valley below.) The path bears right following a contour of the hillside through woodland. Go up more steps as the trees thin out. At a kissing gate marking a junction of paths, ignore the bridleway to the left and continue into open flowery chalk downland with views over reservoirs in the valley of another spur of the Chilterns.

A little further on, there is a view below of the National Trust's **Pitstone Windmill** – *dated 1627, it is the oldest suriving mill in the country – and in the distance among the trees rises the stately bulk of Mentmore House.*

The track goes steadily up **Pitstone Hill** to a wooden marker post indicating the path straight ahead. The view opens up now on the right towards the **Monument**, with woods and dramatic hills and coombes all around. The route begins to descend to a crossing of paths.

 6

(The path straight on leads to the National Trust parking area just off a metalled lane – **Stocks Road** leading from Aldbury – which is part of the route of the **Icknield Way**. Over the road is a signpost to **Ivinghoe Beacon**, 1.4 miles ahead, if you want to extend the walk.) Otherwise, turn right over a stile to leave the **Ridgeway**.

To join the walk if you have parked here, go through the kissing gate from the car park and walk up the hill, forking left at a post and then turning left off the **Ridgeway** over a stile.

 7

Walk along a field edge with a fence on the right. When the fence ends bear half-left over a field, making for a tree-lined field edge ahead. The path crosses a field boundary, continues over a farm track and then over the corner of the next field. Follow the arrow marker left and then right along a hedged boundary to come out onto **Stocks Road**.

 8

Cross a stile and turn right along this narrow lane with billowing hedges on both sides.

Drive and Stroll

(For a SHORT CUT, follow Stocks Road all the way back into **Aldbury**, passing **Stocks**, a mid-Georgian property which belonged to the popular Edwardian novelist Mrs Humphrey Ward. She was a granddaughter of Dr Arnold, the famous headmaster of Rugby school. There is a chequered brick dovecote of 1753 in the farmyard opposite.)

To follow the main walk, having passed a left turn to **Barley End**, continue on to the flint wall of the **Walled Garden**.

Just before this, turn left off the lane (signpost) and through a metal gate into a stableyard. Beyond the stableyard keep ahead, following the bends of a broad track with a field on the left and a hedgerow and woodland on the right. Ignore footpaths crossing the track and continue into the woods of **Ashridge**, bearing to the right to walk in the lee of hanging woodland on the left along a good stony path going steadily uphill.

*At a signpost, the left fork goes uphill towards the **Bridgewater***

***Monument** and can be followed as an extension to this walk. A National Trust kiosk nearby offers snacks on summer weekends.*

Otherwise, continue on along the lower path, passing **Tim's Spring** and then another dwelling on the right. Just after this, turn off the main gravelly track, which bears left, and carry on along an unmarked path through trees and clearings. This path heads downhill through woodland masking **Aldbury** in the valley below. Come out at a footpath on the left. Bear right here along a broader track going downhill to a marker post. Fork right downhill, staying on the main path at two signposts as it goes downhill alongside houses to a road.

Turn right here for the short distance back to the village green.

The **Valiant Trooper** pub is a little way down **Trooper Road** on the left. It has small old-fashioned bars, a large restaurant in a converted barn, and plenty of tables in the garden. It serves excellent food and real ales except on Sunday evenings. Telephone: 01442 851203.

Places of Interest Nearby

The Walter Rothschild Zoological Museum is in Tring, 3½ miles to the east (telephone: 020 7942 6171), and nearby **Tring Park** provides 300 acres of excellent walking (telephone: 01422 823347).

4 Sarratt

This pub dates back to 1739

Distance 3 miles   **Terrain** Undulating
Map OS Explorer Chiltern Hills East 172 (GR 043993)

How to get there

From the A41 turn onto the B4505 on the outskirts of Hemel Hempstead, turning off to follow the signs to Sarratt through Bovingdon and Chipperfield. **Parking**: There is generally plenty of parking on the slip roads next to the village green.

Drive and Stroll

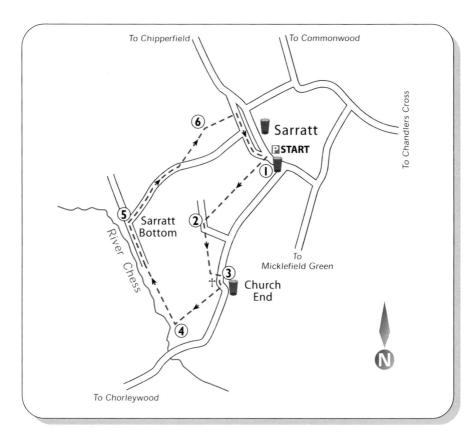

To Chipperfield
To Commonwood
To Chandlers Cross
Sarratt
START
Sarratt Bottom
River Chess
To Micklefield Green
Church End
To Chorleywood
N

Introduction

The little river Chess forms the border between Buckinghamshire and Hertfordshire in the south-west of the county, and the villages which climb the slopes of the valley are especially pretty. Our starting point, Sarratt, with its long, hummocky green, duck ponds, and unusual pump, is a fine example. The names of the houses round the green recall former businesses – bakehouse, forge, saddlery, and wheelwright – and the green itself was probably a watering place along an old drover's route. The walk, which includes parts of the Chess Valley Walk and the Chiltern Way, crosses meadows to reach the hamlet of Sarratt Church End before descending into the Chess Valley. Continuing along a path parallel to the river, it passes first through watermeadows and then along lanes, to Sarratt Bottom. A pretty ascent through the ancient trees of Dawes Common brings the walker back to Sarratt Green.

Refreshments

Dating back to 1739, **the Boot** is a nice old pub on the green. It serves unpretentious pub food and good beers. Telephone: 01923 262247. **The Cricketers** is at the post office end of the green. It is a Blubeckers eating house, with a wide range of à la carte food and a set menu which is changed regularly. Telephone: 01923 263729. **The Cock Inn** at Sarratt Church End has a cockerel theme inside and a pretty garden, as well as good food. Telephone: 01923 282908.

THE WALK

Follow a footpath next to the **Old Forge** (next to the post office at the south-eastern end of the green), signed to **Church End**. The path leaves an alley and cottages to go along the left-hand boundary of a field, crossing several stiles. Eventually, it goes over a stile to follow a marked path passing through woods before coming out onto a lane.

Cross and take the kissing gate and stile slightly to the left, leading into a large meadow. Keep along a fringe of woodland on the left. When the woodland ends, continue walking diagonally up the field towards the pointed roof of the **church of the Holy Cross**. Go over a stile and through a kissing gate into the churchyard to explore this unusual church.

It stands near a Roman site, and is built mainly of flint and Totternhoe stone, with some Roman brick and chunks of Hertfordshire pudding stone. The saddleback tower is unique in Hertfordshire. Opposite the churchyard, on a bend in the lane, is the 17th century Cock Inn, which was once used as a mortuary for plague victims, who were buried in the adjoining field.

To continue the walk, leave the churchyard near the pretty Gothic almshouses. Cross a drive and go through a kissing gate on a footpath signed to **Chorleywood**. It passes between fences and then crosses the drive to **Goldingtons**, an early 19th century manor house. Go over a stile and follow the hedged boundary. Bear right to a metal fence and follow this downhill towards cottages, with lovely views of the valley of the **river Chess**. Cross a stile to reach a track.

Turn right along the **Chess Valley Walk** (marker post), passing the cottages, and go through a wooden kissing gate into a lovely meadow. Continue parallel to the river. At the

Drive and Stroll

end of the meadow, bear left a little way to a kissing gate at a junction of paths. (A board here describes the lynchets or terraced field systems dating from the 9th century which can be seen in this meadow. They were used for crops or possibly vineyards until the 13th century.) Ignoring the path to the left which crosses the river via footbridges, go through the kissing gate ahead. Ignore the path signed to the right (SHORT CUT back to the village via **Church End**) and continue on ahead along a shady path with a hedge on the left and a wood on the right. The path becomes a lane with cottages on the right (**Sarratt Bottom**) and leads to a junction.

 5

The lane continues ahead, but turn right, uphill, passing a cottage on the right and then following the gentle curves of this hazel-lined lane. Ignore the footpath on the right to Sarratt church. Just past the entrance to **Whiteoaks Farm** on the right, a path is signed left through the beautiful old trees of **Dawes Common**. Take this; then bear right up the track. A major track goes ahead, but veer left to a marker post and then right to continue past a wooden bench. Ignore all minor paths. On reaching a crossing of tracks, ignore the one going left through a kissing gate at a marker post and go a few steps right to another marker post; then go left again to follow the same line as before.

 6

Cross a stile into a field and walk ahead across the corner to a fence and hedge; bear slightly right to walk alongside them. When the fence ends, carry on ahead across another corner of the field to a stile by a wooden gate. Cross this and walk ahead along a laurel-hung path between gardens to reach **Sarratt Green** by a footpath signpost. Turn right to go back to the start.

Place of Interest Nearby

Chenies Manor, just over the border near Amersham in Buckinghamshire, is a Tudor house, once home to the Dukes of Bedford, and has beautiful gardens. Telephone: 01494 762888.

5 Aldenham

The church of St John the Baptist at Aldenham

Distance 4 miles   **Terrain** Undulating
Map OS Explorer 173 London North just onto 182 St Albans and Hatfield (GR 145984)

How to get there

The Round Bush is just off the B462, about 1½ miles south-west of Radlett on the A5183. **Parking**: On the quiet road near the pub, or by the green near Aldenham church.

Drive and Stroll

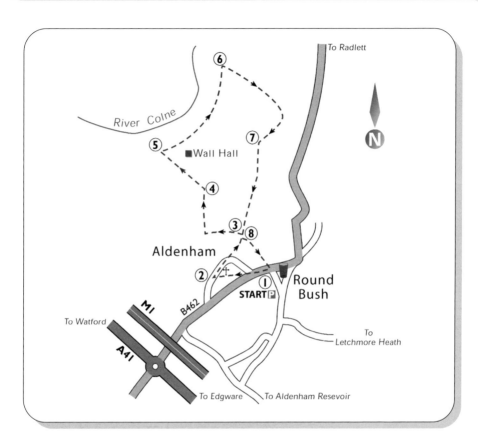

Introduction

Bounded by urban development near the outskirts of London and edged to the west by the M1 and to the east by Watling Street, the villages and hamlets in this small area of countryside are nevertheless singularly unspoilt. The reservoirs of Hillfield Park (a Herts and Middlesex Wildlife Trust reserve), and Aldenham Country Park to the south and the rivers Ver and Colne to the north and west of the walk provide wildlife interest. There are several notable houses in the area, of which Wall Hall and Munden House are passed en route. From the Round Bush pub in the hamlet of the same name, the route follows footpaths past Aldenham's church of St John the Baptist, making for the river via the grounds of ancient Wall Hall, where remnants of the grounds landscaped by Repton can still be seen. Field tracks with good views take the walker back to the pub. This route includes part of the Hertfordshire Way and the Ver-Colne Valley Walk.

Refreshments

The Round Bush, at the start of the walk, is a cosy pub with a pleasant garden for alfresco eating. It offers a lunchtime bar menu and an evening restaurant menu from Wednesday to Saturday. Conveniently, it opens at 9.30 am for breakfast and goes on to offer coffee and snacks before lunch. Telephone: 01923 855532.

THE WALK

Turn right out of the pub and walk to the main road; cross. Turn left along the pavement to reach a road junction where a right turn goes off to **Aldenham**. Over the turn, just by the sign for **Church Lane** is a track with a reflector post. Walk along this fenced and hedged track into **St John's** churchyard. Walk beside an old red brick wall to the church.

The 13th century tower contains lumps of Hertfordshire pudding stone, and though damaged in the Second World War, it now has an elegant spire. Inside are a number of 15th to 16th century brasses and some interesting monuments. Nearby are the Georgian vicarage and farm occupying the site of a Saxon church built by King Offa of Mercia in AD 785.

Pass the church on the right to come out through a gate onto a road at the green in **Aldenham**.

Bear right along the road. Pass the social club and then turn left up a small lane by **Jubilee Cottages**. Keep ahead at white cottages on the left and go into a field, walking along the hedgerow on the right to a cross track in the middle of the field.

Turn left (arrow-marked) and walk through the middle of the field to a driveway with the high-rise buildings of Watford in the distance. Turn right here to reach a new development of houses associated with **Wall Hall**.

The Gothic revival front of this old mansion was added in 1802. There is a ruined folly created from old sections of Aldenham church.

Where the road forks take the right-hand fork and go on to a road junction; take the second left turn, walking along a pavement beside a strip of woodland on the left, with houses on the right. At a road junction go ahead by an iron gate (arrow marker on wooden fencing) onto a broad gravelly track going gently downhill through lovely parkland trees with views of **Wall Hall** on the right and a golf course on the left.

Drive and Stroll

 5

At a crossroads of tracks, ignore the path ahead over a bridge and ford to the **river Colne**. (There was once an ornamental bridge here over a lake, part of the landscaped gardens.) Turn right along a good gravelled track through woodland on the right and meadows leading to woodland on the left. Pass a gate on the right and continue; on the left, through an extensive plantation of trees, are views of late Victorian **Munden House** on the valley slope.

 6

Just by the gate to **River Lodge** on the left, take a broad leafy unsigned lane to the right which goes under power lines and snakes its way uphill, eventually passing a sewage plant to reach a cross track by farm buildings. Turn right along a broad track, avoiding a lane to the left, and go through by the buildings of **Blackbird's Farm** (yellow arrow marker on a red brick building to the right); bear slightly left through the farmyard and go on to a wide gravelly track.

 7

After a short distance, there is a big opening by a metal gate on the left. Here a narrow grassy path goes left off the wide track into a field. Keep ahead along this (marker on kissing gate), with a hedgerow to the left. Towards the end of the field, curve slightly right to a kissing gate marked with an arrow. From there continue along the next field, going under power lines. Walk in the same direction as before with a copse on the left to another kissing gate, which offers a good view of **Aldenham** church. Go into the next field, where halfway down there is a crossing of tracks.

 8

The outward journey took the right turn across the field here; the return journey goes left over a stile (marked with an arrow) and bears half right over a meadow, going over a stile and towards white gates. Go across a cricket field, following the same line. A few yards to the right of the white gates, go through a wooden gate with a signpost and come out onto the main road. Turn left along the pavement to return to the pub in **Round Bush Lane**.

Place of Interest Nearby

Aldenham Country Park, near Elstree, has a rare breeds farm as well as woodland trails and lakeside walks. Telephone: 020 8953 9602.

6 Little Berkhamsted

St Andrew's church, Little Berkhamsted, dates from 1647

Distance 4 miles   **Terrain** Undulating
Map OS Explorer 182 St Albans and Hatfield (GR 292079)

How to get there

Turn off the A414 between Hertford and Hatfield onto the B1455 and then onto the B158, signed to Essendon. Go through Essendon; Little Berkhamsted is signed to the left. **Parking**: Near the church or the pub in Church Road, Little Berkhamsted, which is reached by turning off Berkhamsted Road at the war memorial; alternatively, unless there is a function, outside Essendon village hall in School Lane.

Drive and Stroll

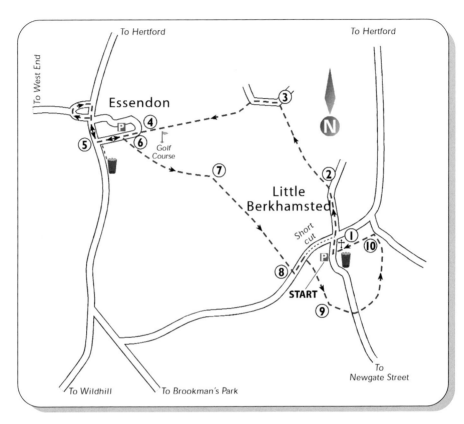

Introduction

The rolling woods and meadows in the Lea valley between Little Berkhamsted and Essendon form an oasis of relatively unspoilt territory in the mainly urban south-eastern corner of Hertfordshire. Little Berkhamsted was the early home of the cricket commentator Brian Johnston, who was born in the Old Rectory, and the circus boss Bertram Mills lived in New Manor during the Second World War. In addition to the Old Rectory, which was built in 1737 on Robin's Nest Hill to replace a Tudor building, Little Berkhamsted also has the New Rectory of 1896, in adjoining Breach Lane, and the present rectory, a modern bungalow in Berkhamsted Lane. Essendon is a tight knot of houses and cottages near the church, with several gracious old houses dotted around the countryside of the parish. The walk, partly along the Hertfordshire Way, explores the wooded valley between the two villages, using shady old lanes, field paths, and a golf course near quarry workings.

Refreshments

Little Berkhamsted's Five Horseshoes is a Chef and Brewer pub, which is open all day every day. The low-beamed ceilings inside are hung with hops, and there is a pleasant little garden with tables. The menu is varied, and specials are offered. Telephone: 01707 875055.

THE WALK

Walk a few steps to the main road near the war memorial (where Berkhamsted Lane becomes Robin's Nest Hill) and turn right for a short distance. Turn left down **Breach Lane**, with New Rectory on the right.

*Through a gap on the right of this broad, leafy lane, there is a glimpse of **Stratton's Folly**, a 100-ft red brick tower built in 1789 by John Stratton, a retired admiral, so that he could see the shipping on the Thames.*

Before long look for an opening into a field on the left (arrow marker on post). Turn left off the lane and bear half right over a field, descending towards a knot of woodland. Cross the bridge in the corner of the field and continue down an ancient track through some lovely old trees. (Near the bottom, a stile on the right leads into a field where access is allowed under the Countryside Stewardship scheme.) The walk, however, continues down the track to come out onto a lane

by **Ashfield Farm** and an enormous old oak tree.

Ignore the footpath ahead and turn left along the lane, passing scattered cottages. Almost opposite **Ashfield House** on the right, bear left off the lane along a track with quarry workings to the right. Keep along the main track, crossing a ditch and going over a cross track (metal barrier on right). Carry on through wooden posts onto a golf course (arrow markers). This is the Hatfield London Country Club. Cross over a bridge with a pond on the right and continue ahead along a hard track with stretches of gravel. Go gently uphill towards scattered conifers. Eventually the path goes through a wooden barrier and alongside **Essendon** school to come to a roadway at a footpath signpost.

Bear left up the road (**School Lane**), passing modern housing on the right. Soon on the left is a footpath signpost. This is the return route to Little Berkhamsted (point 6), which can be taken if you do not want to explore **Essendon**. Otherwise, pass the village hall on

Drive and Stroll

the right (with alternative parking).

Turn right along **High Road** into the village.

*To visit the **Rose and Crown** pub, go left. This pub offers simple food and friendly service. As well as a dining room, it has a dining terrace and a garden. Food is not available on Sunday and Monday evenings. Telephone: 01707 261229.*

*At the war memorial bear left along Church Street, passing **St Mary's church**, which was restored in 1883. Its chief glory is an unusual Wedgwood black basalt font, donated in the 1770s by Mary Whitbread, of the brewing family, who lived at nearby Bedwell Park. There are also some interesting memorials.*

*The lane to the left leads to a former pub, the ancient **Salisbury Crest**, a reminder of the village's connection with the Salisbury family of nearby Hatfield House.*

To resume the walk, turn right to the main road; then turn right again along the main road and left down **School Lane**.

Halfway down, take a path to the right, signed to **Little Berkhamsted**. As a gated drive swings right, the path bears left downhill through scattered trees, including some impressive old oaks. Negotiate a gap in wooden posts next to a white barrier to go back onto the golf course. Go straight ahead across a fairway, passing a small lake and then the clubhouse with its terrace and conservatory. Bear right round the corner here (marker post) and then left again (marker post) to go downhill, passing another pond to reach a machinery shed on the left. Continue through a metal gate (marker post) at a crossing of paths.

Carry straight on past a cottage on the right, going through wooden fencing, marked with an arrow, and then uphill through woodland. Come out through a gap into more open countryside with fields and woods to left and right. When the woodland ends, the path passes through fenced-off fields with a view of turreted **Bedwell Park** over the valley on the hillside. Continue through a kissing gate next to a metal gate, pass huge barns on the left, and walk along a driveway leading to a house on the right. Come out at a gatehouse.

Turn left along the lane for a short distance. (For a SHORT CUT continue along the lane back to Little Berkhamsted.)

Otherwise, turn right off the lane into an opening with a metal gate by a bridleway signpost. Go through the gap by the gate and alongside fencing on the right. Ignore a kissing gate to the left leading across to the pub and continue along the edge of another fenced-off field looking down into a valley on the right.

 9

Before the next section of bridleway, take a footpath to the left through the hedgerow (arrow-marked) and bear half right across a field to a kissing gate. Through the gate, continue on the same line towards a metal gate and signpost in a hedge. Go through and cross the road, continuing through another metal gate and along a path signed to **Buck's Alley**. Walk along the edge of a field with a hedge and trees on the right, bearing slightly right between a scrappy hedgerow on the left and a fence (arrow-marked) leading down to lovely wooded slopes. **Stratton's Folly** comes into view again. Ignore footpaths to right and then left and carry on through a

metal kissing gate into woodland. Follow a grassy path going downhill into a field, ignoring tracks off. Keeping along the right-hand boundary, go through into the next field by an arrow marker and make for the house ahead.

 10

At the corner there is an exit into Buck's Alley, but our route turns left here, along a hedgerow, and then goes through a kissing gate into another field, making for cottages ahead. Pass the churchyard on the right, to come out onto **Church Road** through a kissing gate.

St Andrew's church, built in 1647 but heavily restored in Victorian times, has an altar of around 1890 commemorating Bishop Ken, who was chaplain to Charles II and was born in the village in 1637. He had family links to Isaak Walton, author of The Compleat Angler. *There is also a memorial stone to Oliver Cromwell's grandson.*

Place of Interest Nearby

As well as the zoo, the **Paradise Wildlife Park** 3½ miles east of Little Berkhamsted has rides and an adventure playground. Telephone: 01992 470490.

7 | Hertingfordbury

The old mill in Hertingfordbury

Distance 2½ miles   **Terrain** Gentle hills
Maps OS Explorer 174 Epping Forest and Lea Valley, 182 St Albans and Hertford (GR 308119).

How to get there

From the A414 south of Hertford, turn off at a roundabout and follow the signs to Hertingfordbury. **Parking**: In the road outside the church in St Mary's Lane, which forks off the main street; alternatively, at a small railway bridge past the church where there is parking on the left for the Cole Green Way.

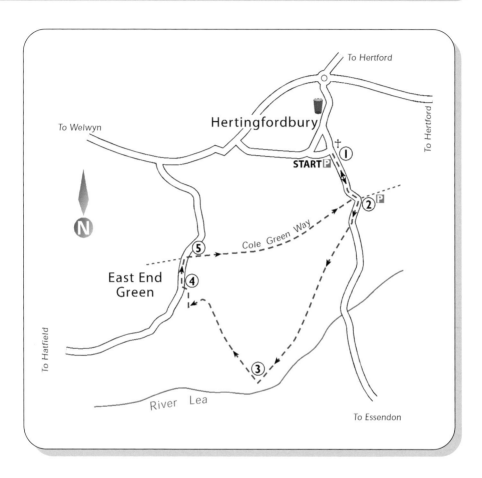

Introduction

Pretty Hertingfordbury, the site of a late Saxon settlement, nestles between the valleys of the rivers Mimram and Lea. It has several interesting buildings including an 18th century watermill, an old coaching inn, and a 13th century church. To the north are lovely beech woods which fringe the Panshanger estate, designed in 1801 by Humphrey Repton for the 5th Earl Cowper. The ancient landscape has been irrevocably changed though by gravel workings, and the 19th century mansion was demolished in 1954. The walk follows wooded footpaths, passing through historic Grotto Wood, to the hamlet of East End Green. It then takes advantage of the Cole Green Way, a good path along a former railway line, from Letty Green back to Hertingfordbury.

Drive and Stroll

Refreshments

The White Horse Hotel was once an old timbered coaching inn dating back to the 16th century. It was given a Georgian façade and now has a modern extension. It offers a reasonable bar menu, plus sandwiches, salads, and baguettes, in its comfortable leather-seated bar areas or pleasant garden. There is an evening restaurant menu. Outside, an interesting information board records the history of the village. Telephone: 0870 400 8114.

THE WALK

From the churchyard, turn left and walk up the lane to the **Cole Green Way** parking area.

*The **church of St Mary with St John** had connections with John of Gaunt and to this day the patronage belongs to the Duchy of Lancaster (i.e. the Crown). It was renovated in 1890 by the Cowpers, who added a chapel to house their family monuments spanning three centuries.*

From the bridge, walk along the main road for a little way. Just past the delimit signs, turn right along a broad bridleway, walking past a metal barrier and then alongside fencing and woodland. Continue gently uphill for some distance.

*There are wide views over the **Lea valley** on the left, and on the hillside **Bayfordbury House**, an imposing Regency building, with its 18th century landscaped grounds and an important pinetum of later date.*

Carry on through woodland, going gently downhill until the woods thin out and old, moated Roxford Farm, its buildings, and finally a white cottage appear on the left.

At a wooden footpath signpost, turn right along a footpath to **East End Green**, ignoring the route to the left to Water Hall. Take the right hand route through a kissing gate next to a wooden farm gate and go uphill along a broad gravelly track between a hedge and a fenced field. The track bears to the right, signed to **Grotto Wood**, which is accessed through a kissing gate.

The information board reveals that this was once part of a formal late 17th to early 18th century garden with ponds and a grotto, which belonged to an earlier manor house on the site of Roxford Farm.

It is possible to walk through the wood and pick up the walk on the other side. Alternatively, turn right, and then, ignoring a permissive path ahead at gravel workings, bear left along a fenced-off footpath alongside the wood to a junction of paths. Turn left along the top end of the wood, ignoring the footpath which goes straight on. There is a kissing gate where the path through the wood emerges. The fenced footpath comes out through a wooden barrier (arrow-marked) and crosses a roadway leading into the gravel workings. On the other side, go through a kissing gate and carry on ahead between a tall hedge and a fence towards the houses of **East End Green**. At a T-junction of tracks, turn right a short way; bear left at the corner where another track comes in from the right; and almost immediately come to a lane at **East End Green**.

The White Horse hotel dates back to the 16th century

 (4)

Turn right along the lane, ignoring a footpath off to the left. Just after a house called **Hazeldene** on the left, the lane goes over the **Cole Green Way**. This route for walkers, cyclists, and riders follows the course of a disused railway line, once the branch line from **Welwyn Garden City** to **Hertford** and now a valuable wildlife habitat. (If you walk to the left, you reach **Letty Green** and **The Cowper Arms** pub.)

 (5)

Go down the slope onto the old railway track and turn right. From here back to the parking place is a straightforward enjoyable walk along the track, sometimes through cuttings and sometimes on embankments above the countryside. Beyond the bridge over the road back to **Hertingfordbury**, is the former station and platform, now converted into The Old Station House. Go down steps by the bridge to the parking area and back along the road to the church.

Place of Interest Nearby

Hertford Museum of local history, in the town of Hertford, has a Jacobean style garden. Telephone: 01992 582686.

8 St Albans

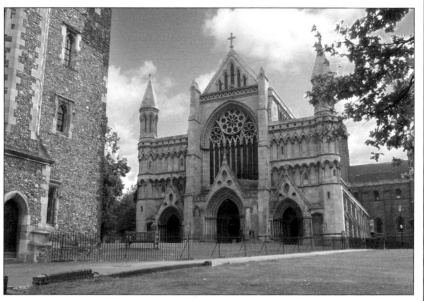

St Alban's Abbey was built in 1077

Distance 2, 3½ or 5 miles **Terrain** Undulating
Map OS Explorer 182 St Albans and Hatfield (GR 136073)

How to get there

From the A1(M), Junction 3, at Hatfield follow signs to St Albans (A414, A1081). **Parking**: In the city follow signs to Verulamium, go over the main crossroads, and then, avoiding the A5183 right to Redbourn, carry straight on down narrow streets (cathedral on left) into Fishpool Street. At the bottom, turn left and left again into the large pay-and-display car park (with toilets) by Verulamium Museum. Alternatively, this can be reached from the A4147 Hemel Hempstead road by turning into St Michael's Street opposite the Roman Theatre. It pays to arrive early as it can get busy.

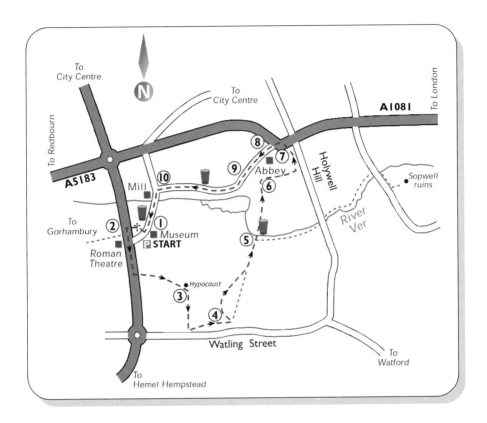

Introduction

There are few cities in or on the edge of glorious parkland and countryside where you can find such a wealth of fascinating history and archaeology. Add in numerous lovely pubs, cafés, and restaurants and you have the ingredients for a magical day out. St Albans is at the crossroads of several Roman roads, and today several walking routes meet here.

This walk follows parts of the Hertfordshire Way, the Ver-Colne Valley Walk, and the Alban Way through the green heart of this city. From Verulamium Park, which has wildlife-rich expanses of woodland, meadowland, and water, the walk explores several stretches of the wall of Verulamium, Roman Britain's third largest town. From the park, the walker climbs up to the great cathedral and abbey church containing the shrine of St Alban, Britain's first Christian martyr, and the domestic architecture of Fishpool Street and St Michael's village provide an interesting finale to this varied walk.

Drive and Stroll

For a greater challenge, the walk can be extended at two points: the first leads to a Roman theatre and to the 18th century mansion of Gorhambury, and the ruins of Elizabethan Old Gorhambury, and a second detour takes in the haunting ruins of Sopwell Nunnery.

Refreshments

The Six Bells in St Michael's village, on a former coaching route, stands on the remains of a Roman bathhouse. It offers good food and traditional ales, and is open all day on Saturday and Sunday. No food is available on Sunday or Monday evenings. Telephone: 01727 856945.

THE WALK

From the museum (which is full of fascinating finds from Verulamium, including wonderful mosaics and recreated Roman rooms), turn right for a short distance, and then bear left through the gates of **St Michael's church**.

Built on the site of a Roman cemetery, St Michael's houses a marble effigy of Sir Francis Bacon (died 1626), Lord Keeper of the Great Seal.

Follow the main path round the church to come out on **Bluehouse Hill** (A4147).

*To visit the **Roman theatre** and Gorhambury (about 2 miles there and back), bear right to the junction and cross the road. The theatre is just inside the gates to Gorhambury. Nearby are ground markings of a 2nd or 3rd century town house with an underground shrine and shops facing onto Watling Street. It was probably destroyed by Boudicca in her fight against the Roman invaders. From here a permissive footpath along the estate drive leads to **Gorhambury House** (1777–84), open on Thursday afternoons only, and the ruins of the Tudor mansion of **Old Gorhambury**, (the home of the Bacon family). Retrace your steps.*

To continue the main walk: leaving St Michael's churchyard, turn left along the main road, passing the vicarage grounds (the site of the Roman forum). Soon after, turn left through a gap in fencing into Verulamium Park. Follow a grassy path ahead (bearing very slightly right) over meadowland and go through a hedgerow into the park proper. The museum and car park are way over on the left and there is a good view of the cathedral ahead. Make for a flint-walled structure ahead and go up steps to the right to a white modern building protecting a mosaic floor and the hypocaust of a large villa (AD 180).

3

Come out of the building by the same door and turn right uphill towards trees across open grassland, making in the general direction of a dog waste bin. Before reaching a way through to King Harry Lane, turn left along a mown path towards trees, following the course of the Roman city wall indicated by mounds and ditches. Follow the mown path downhill between trees with a deep wooded ditch on the left. Just before trees ahead, bear left along their edge and then right into woodland.

 4

Walk uphill, bearing right to go through woodland along a path on top of the mound of the wall. Carry straight on for some distance, bearing left as the path goes downhill with the hummock of a wall on the right, some of it exposed. As you leave the woodland, the end of the lake (the site of a Roman cemetery) is ahead.

*It is worth turning back on yourself to the right along **The Causeway**, a path passing the remains of the south-eastern gate, where Watling Street entered the city, to follow a large exposed section of Roman wall towards the site of the south tower.*

Retrace your footsteps and continue down the hard path to a crossroads of tracks with a hedge coming in from the left. Over on the left is

another large section of wall and the site of **St Germain's Priory**, built in AD 256-70. Carry on along the end of the lake, passing a Hertfordshire Way sign and then toilets on the right.

*To follow part of the **Ver-Colne Valley Walk** to the ruins of **Sopwell Nunnery** (1½ miles return trip), go off at a right angle behind the toilet block, down steps, and walk along the bank of the willow hung river Ver. Cross over **Holywell Hill** and pass through a gap between brick pillars. Continue along a narrow track beside the river, crossing over a footbridge to walk with the river now on the right. Eventually go up steps to **Cottonmill Lane**. Turn right, pass a lane called Old Sopwell Gardens, and then go left over a green area to the ruins of **Sopwell Nunnery** (1571), also called Lee Hall after its builder. The ruins are those of a Tudor mansion built on the site of an earlier medieval nunnery established in 741 and dissolved in 1537.*

Retrace your steps to the lake.

 5

Walk ahead, crossing the **river Ver** near **The Olde Fighting Cocks** inn on the right (telephone: 01727 869152).

The octagonal section of the pub was originally a medieval pigeon house, re-erected on the site of a monastery founded in 793 by Offa

Drive and Stroll

of Mercia. In the 17th and 18th century the place was a venue for cock fighting and it is probably the oldest inhabited inn in the country.

Carry on up **Abbey Mill Lane** towards the abbey gateway, erected in the 1360s, which has connections with the Peasant's Revolt, was used as a prison for three centuries, and is now part of St Alban's School.

The Black Lion Inn, St Albans

 6

Just before gateway, turn right into the grounds of **St Alban's Abbey**. The abbey was built in 1077 (with later additions), and the tower contains Roman bricks.

*Walk round the abbey to the right, going under the arch of the modern chapter house; bear left, and then right, round a magnificent cedar tree planted in 1803 by the 1st Earl Spencer. At the east end of the cathedral, you can go through **Sumpter Yard** to reach the shops and cafés of **Holywell Hill**.*

 7

To continue the walk, come back towards the east end of the cathedral and bear right up steps leading into peaceful **Vintry Garden**, where once the abbey vineyard

flourished. Cross the garden to a gate in the wall on the other side, which leads along an alley and through **Waxhouse Gate** into **High Street**, where the early 15th century clock tower faces you. It is the only medieval town belfry in England, and Gabriel, its original bell, is still in place.

 8

Turn back along the alley, keeping the wall of the Vintry Garden on the left. Turn right through a gate and walk along the north side of the abbey. Go ahead through gates, cross the road (**Romeland**), and bear left through the small garden here, which commemorates the burning on this site of George Tankerfield, a protestant martyr in reign of Mary Tudor.

 9

Come out onto the street and continue down **Fishpool Street**, near the abbey fishponds, with its amazing variety of interesting and attractive domestic architecture from several centuries.

Turn at the bottom of the street, cross over **Branch Road**.

*Opposite is **Kingsbury Water Mill Museum**, a restored and working mill dating from the 16th century with its own restaurant and café, called the Waffle. Note the lump of Hertfordshire pudding stone outside. Telephone: 01727 853502.*

The ruins of Sopwell Nunnery, also called Lee Hall after its builder

Turn left and cross the **river Ver** over **St Michael's Bridge**, alongside the 2000-year-old ford.

There was a causeway when the Romans arrived in AD 43, and a bridge was first built in the 3rd century. Opposite Prae Close, a gate takes the Ver-Colne Valley Walk into Verulamium Park and beside river and lake back to The Olde Fighting Cocks inn (see point 5 above).

The walk continues up **St Michael's Street**, passing more ancient buildings, including the **Rose and Crown** and the **Six Bells** pubs, and, on the left, **Darrowfield House**, an early 18th century chequered brick building, which was once the dower house for Gorhambury. Turn left off the main road to return to the parking place.

Place of Interest Nearby

The **Verulamium Museum** of everyday life in Roman Britain, in St Albans, is set in parkland with Roman remains. Telephone: 01727 751810.

9 Much Hadham and Perry Green

Morris Cottage, Much Hadham, was home to William

Distance 5 miles   **Terrain** Hilly
Map OS Explorer 194 Hertford and Bishops Stortford (GR 428197)

How to get there

From the A10 take the A120 road towards Bishop's Stortford. Shortly, by the Bell pub in Standon, turn right to Much Hadham, following a winding lane for about 3 miles. Turn right at a T-junction into the village. **Parking**: In the main street near the turning to the church.

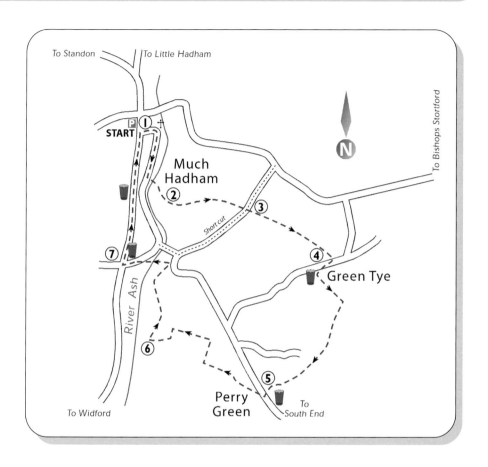

Introduction

This walk makes the most of the beautiful countryside in the east of the county towards the border with Essex. From Much Hadham, with its handsome High Street, the walk goes uphill through fields to reach the hamlet of Green Tye and then takes more field paths to arrive at Perry Green, where, from a public footpath through the grounds of the late Henry Moore's home, some of his imposing sculptures can be seen in a garden setting. Sloping fields and old woodland alongside the valley of the river Ash, take the walker back into Much Hadham and its ancient dwellings. Much Hadham was an important place in earliest times, linked with Hadda, a Saxon warrior who successfully fought the Danes outside neighbouring Widford.

Drive and Stroll

Refreshments

The Hoops Inn in Perry Green has good food and plenty of covered outdoor seating. Telephone: 01279 843568. Other pubs close by include the **Prince of Wales** freehouse in Green Tye which has an attractive garden (telephone: 01279 841041); and in Much Hadham, there is the **Old Crown**, a friendly family owned freehouse (telephone: 01279 842753), and the **Bull Inn**, a country pub with a pretty courtyard garden and good food (telephone: 01279 842668).

THE WALK

Turn down **Church Lane** and walk along the lime-tree avenue to the church.

Later styles have largely masked the 12th century origin of **St Andrew's church**. The 14th century arches have highly decorative capitals; the screen and pulpit are 15th century, and there are some interesting brasses. A pair of heads by Henry Moore flank the tower doorway.

Behind the church is the 16th century former old palace of the bishops of London. In AD 946 a Saxon queen left her lands here to the bishops of London, and a summer palace was built. Here, 500 years later, Katherine, the widow of Henry V, gave birth to her bastard son. He was to be the father of Henry VII.

Turn right round the corner by the church and continue along the lane, lined at first with cottages and then with greenery and a ditch or stream on the left. Ignoring the footpath left to Winding Hill, carry on to where the lane bends to the right. Here, just past a house called **Two Bridges**, go left through a kissing gate (signpost) and over a bridge; then bear right along an obvious path through a meadow.

Bear left and go through a kissing gate by the gates to **Little Hill**. Then go over a drive and into a meadow, turning left uphill alongside the drive. Go through another kissing gate and continue ahead, passing a house behind a hedge on the left. Go through another kissing gate onto a broad track. Go left for a short distance; then turn right into a field through an unmarked gap in the hedge. Pass a house and walk ahead along the right-hand boundary of an arable field, with a ditch on the right. About halfway down, go through a gap in the hedge and cross the ditch (no bridge). Bear left, walking ahead again, this time with the boundary on your left, to meet **Danebridge Lane** at a metal signpost.

(For a SHORT CUT, turn right to return to Much Hadham.)

 (3)

Cross the lane and go up the signed track opposite between houses and gardens. At the end of a paddock, turn left (wooden signpost) alongside a wooden paddock fence. Follow the narrow path which bears to the right beside a stream to come out into a field beyond a knot of woodland. Continue on along the right-hand boundary of the field. The boundary hedge and stream bear right to the end of a hedgerow, where a footbridge takes a bridleway off to the right. The walk bears left and continues along the field boundary in the same direction as before (no marker posts). There are glasshouses over the field on the right. This fieldside path goes on for some distance towards a knot of trees and a building. Keep on alongside a hedged paddock, with a field now on the right. Leave the field at a marker post by a pretty boarded cottage. Ignoring the path to the right, carry on to the road and the large green at **Green Tye**, surrounded by weatherboarded houses.

 (4)

Walk to the right along the road, ignoring a footpath to the right and passing a pond. Immediately before the **Prince of Wales** pub (telephone: 01279 841041), turn left along a broad byway (signed from the right-hand side of the road), passing

A Henry Moore sculpture seen from the footpath

cottages. Where a drive sweeps right, keep ahead along a smaller muddy track between hedges. At a T-junction of tracks, go right into a field and walk alongside the hedgerow on the right (no signs). Keep on along the hedgerow and then beside a wooden fence and ditch, with good views on the left. Bear left at the end of the fence (arrow marker) and carry on along another hedgerow and ditch. When the hedge ends, continue along the edge of this field towards a farmyard. The track skirts the yard of **Bucklers Hall Farm** to arrive at a footpath marker post. Ignoring the byway left, continue, bearing slightly right and passing farm hard-standing. At another marker post, continue to bear right along the boundary of the field, with a pond or moat on the right and the early 17th century farmhouse beyond. When the hedgerow ends continue following the ditch as it curves along the edge of the field towards trees and a cottage. A marker post points right along the contours of the field. Kink right and then left, finally

Drive and Stroll

bearing right by a white cottage (marker post) to come out onto **Perry Green**. The **Hoops Inn** is down the lane on the left.

 (5)

Cross the green and the road and follow the signed route along the drive to **Dane Tree House** (formerly Hoglands), the home of the Henry Moore Foundation, passing the house and studios on the left and going through a white wicket gate. At a bend in the drive, the footpath is signed ahead over a stile by a metal gate. It bears right along the ridged edge of a field. Cross another stile by a metal gate and continue past farm buildings. Go through a metal gate (signed) and walk between fields. Before the track meets another metal gate, go right (signpost) along a good grassy track between fields to another signpost, which indicates left. Go downhill here towards woodland, where an arrow marker points left. Soon, at another arrow marker, turn right alongside the woodland and go downhill, crossing a stile to another arrow marker at a junction of paths.

 (6)

Turn right along a track (part of the Hertfordshire Way), eventually walking alongside steep **Sidehill Wood**. Further on the path goes steeply down to a lane (signpost). Turn left for a short distance to the corner; then go left through a kissing gate into a field. Bear left across the meadow towards the houses and cottages of **Much Hadham**. Cross the river by means of a concrete bridge and continue. Go through a metal kissing gate onto **Malting Lane**. Bear left and then right round the corner to reach the main road.

 (7)

Turn right along here (**Tower Hill**).

The walk passes a decorative Victorian brick **Congregational church** and **Morris Cottage** which was the home of William Morris's sister. Tower Hill runs into **High Street**, where, on the left, is the **Forge Museum**. Cross over another little lane to reach the brick wall protecting **Much Hadham Hall** (circa 1727), connected with Walter de la Mare. **The Collarmaker's House** and weatherboarded **Chancery Cottage** are on the left. The beamed **Rectory** and gabled new **Manor House** are on the right.

Place of Interest Nearby

The Henry Moore Foundation, at Perry Green about 2 miles to the south-east, has gardens, studios and changing exhibitions. Telephone: 01279 843333.

10 Watton at Stone

The church of St Mary, Stapleford

Distance 4 miles   **Terrain** Mostly level
Map OS Explorer 194 Hertford and Bishops Stortford (GR 303193)

How to get there

Watton at Stone is signed off the A602 Stevenage to Ware road. **Parking**: In the lay-bys near the Bull Inn in Watton at Stone High Street; please park carefully. Off road parking is also available at Stapleford churchyard.

Drive and Stroll

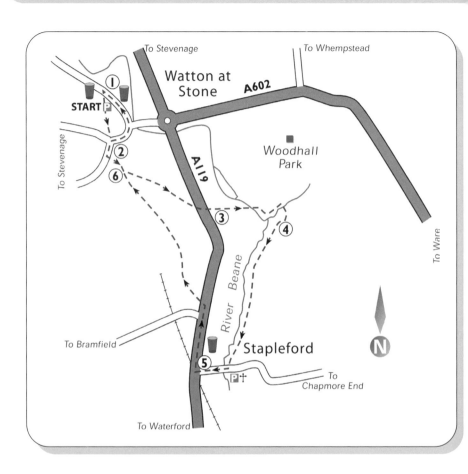

Introduction

The large village of Watton at Stone, between Stevenage and Hertford, is built on the site of a Roman camp, and many Roman remains, including over 100 gold coins, were uncovered when the bypass was built. There was a great battle between the Saxons and Danes in 1016, and several mounds in the vicinity date from Roman and Saxon times; one excavation revealed the ruin of an old church and the earliest stained glass found in Europe. The village continued to be important in the Middle Ages as part of the chief manor of the Abbot of Westminster. The walk leaves Watton's attractive High Street and wooded lanes to walk through Woodhall Park with its imposing neo-classical house and lovely parkland. Crossing a bridge at the end of the lake created by widening the river Beane – the haunt of many water birds – it then follows the course of the rather depleted river to the village of Stapleford before returning through fields to Watton at Stone.

Refreshments

The Bull is a traditional village pub. It is housed in a listed medieval hall house (telephone: 01920 831032). Also on the High Street is the early 17th century **George and Dragon**, with excellent food (telephone: 01920 830285).

THE WALK

Turn off the **High Street** into **School Lane**, opposite the **Bull pub**. At the school gate, take the hedged footpath to the left, signed to the church.

The church is dedicated to St Andrew and St Mary, and contains nice old stained glass and brasses from 1361 to 1614 as well as Roundhead graffiti. It is said to be haunted by a grey lady.

At the church, bear left down a lane to a junction of roads at a grassy triangle. Bear right up **Perrywood Lane**.

After a short distance, take a path to the left, signed to **Sacombe** and **Stapleford**, passing a farmyard on the left and before long reaching a small wooden gate. Go through this and take a path bearing left through the middle of a field, aiming for a fringe of trees.

*Standing proud on its ridge over on the left is **Woodhall Park** (now a school), which was built in 1777 by Thomas Leverton, the architect of Bedford Square. As well as the outstanding Etruscan saloon and a beautiful staircase hall, it boasts a rare, recently restored print room of 1782.*

Pass over a stile and through a fringe of woodland; over a second stile go on across the middle of a field (marker post). The undulating land offers good views of the house and the cupola of the converted stable block almost hidden in trees. The path comes out on a farm track. Keep along this, eventually passing a cottage on the left to reach a road (A119).

Cross over; go through the gates of **Woodhall Park** by a gatehouse and continue along the drive. Bear right over a bridge over the **river Beane**, where the lake begins to widen (signpost), and continue to the right along the edge of the river, with **Home Farm** and **River House** on

Drive and Stroll

The village pump in the High Street, Watton at Stone

the left. Bear left round farm buildings and then right over another bridge (signpost). The path bends to the right and crosses yet another bridge. Make for a metal fence and go through the remains of an old kissing gate in the middle (signpost). Go gently uphill towards another signpost and continue to a wall, where there is a tall wooden stile (difficult for dogs but there is a gate to the left and a section of barred fence giving alternative access to the footpath).

 4

The fenced path borders the river Beane; continue along it, ignoring a cross track and eventually passing

through some woodland to reach a grassy area bordered by houses. Continue ahead alongside the river; then follow a road (**Clusterbolts**) lined with houses to come out opposite **Stapleford's church of St Mary** with its timbered and lead spired tower and Norman doorway. Here there is an off-road parking area for the **Gravel Walk Nature Trail**. Turn right along the lane over the river and then over a bridged ditch to meet the main road (A119).

 5

Turn right, walking along the pavement, past the houses and cottages of Stapleford and the **Woodhall Arms**, which offers pub and restaurant food, fine ales, and accommodation (telephone: 01992 525123). At the end of the village turn left into **Gobions Lane** and then bear right by a wooden farm gate (signpost to **Watton Green** hidden in the hedge). Go half-left through a field towards **Patchendon Farm**. Climb over a stile and pass between the house and its barns, turning left between a fence and a hedge for a short distance. Turn right into a field (signpost) and continue through the field to another obvious signpost ahead. Go through a gap in the hedgerow and continue over the next field towards a clump of trees (signpost). Continue downhill to a ditch and another signpost. Cross the footbridge and walk up the hillside beyond. Go through a new hedge and a young spinney (signposts); then continue through a field towards the grey roof of a house. (To the right are views of Woodhall Park again.) At the end of the field, cross a farm track, go through at a field boundary, bearing slightly right (signpost),

and then continue ahead up a wide grassy strip with a hedge and trees on the left.

If you have started at Stapleford, you can just turn right here to follow the footpath back through Woodhall Park (see points 2,3 and 4). Otherwise, to return to Watton, go back through the wooden gate taken on the outward leg of the walk, and retrace your steps along the track and out onto the road, bearing right to the church. Here, instead of going back along the track to **School Lane**, go into the churchyard. Bear right past the church and continue downhill, leaving the churchyard through a gate and passing through a meadow onto a road. Here there is a three-way junction, with the war memorial on the left and the Watton village sign over the road. Bear left through overhanging trees back along the **High Street** to the Bull, noting the old milestone on the left and the decorative Victorian almshouses opposite the pub.

Place of Interest Nearby

Fairlands Valley Park is in Stevenage, about 6 miles north-west, and has parkland and a watersports centre. Telephone: 01438 353241.

11 Tewin, Burnham Green and Bull's Green

Elizabethan Queen Hoo Hall, Tewin

Distance 4½ miles **Terrain** Undulating
Map OS Explorer 182 St Albans and Hatfield (GR 271154)

How to get there

From the A1(M) junction 6, follow signs to the B1000 Hertford road. Tewin is signed to the left, beyond Welwyn Garden City. **Parking**: In Upper Green in Tewin, almost opposite the Plume of Feathers, near tennis courts and the playing field (if no matches are taking place). A little further on, along Orchard Road, there is parking on the right if visiting Tewin Orchard Nature Reserve. In Bull's Green where the byway goes left off the road there is parking for a few cars (see point 7).

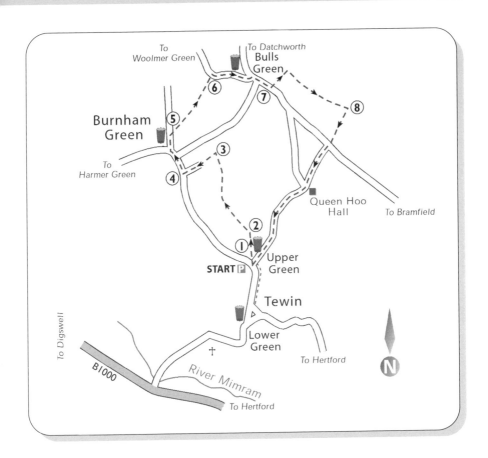

Introduction

This is a walk through woods via various greens, once the only clearings in vast tracts of woodland. An almost triangular route explores this beautiful area, and at every point there is an excellent pub. From Upper Green, Tewin, the walk passes a curious development of inter-war dwellings that has been set down in Panchett's Wood to reach Burnham Green, where a field path, giving views over woodland, makes for the hamlet of Bull's Green, set in tree-lined lanes. Wooded byways lead towards Bramfield Woods before dropping down to Elizabethan Queen Hoo Hall, again through wonderful mixed woodland. Here the walk turns south, down Tewin Hill, at first densely overhung with woodland. A view over to ancient Bramfield Park Wood opens up as the walk descends to Tewin. The woods are especially beautiful in spring when they are carpeted with wild flowers.

Drive and Stroll

Refreshments

The **Plume of Feathers** is a thriving Greene King pub, in Upper Green, Tewin. It has been a great centre for cricket over the years (the cricket pitch is across the road). The inn dates from the 17th century. On offer are good food and beers, and there is a lovely patio and garden (garden games available). Telephone: 01438 717265.

THE WALK

From the parking place, walk the very short distance to the road along a marked track. Cross to the pub, turning left off the road by a footpath signpost, to walk along a hedge on the left. Go left, and then right round the back of the pub along an alley. Go over a stile into a meadow and go straight across the middle towards a hedgerow with a huge tree on the right.

Go through a kissing gate here; ignoring the path straight ahead, bear half-left across the field towards woodland. Go through a gap by a wooden fence (arrow), and walk along a narrow path between the fences and hedges of properties in **Tewin Wood**. The path comes out at a road junction. Take **East Riding** ahead and walk along a street of mixed 1930s' housing in the middle of woodland. Continue for some distance, passing a road going right and then one to the left where **East Riding** becomes **Cowper Way**.

When the road swings sharply right, go ahead along a signed path between houses in woodland.

At an arrow-marked cross track, turn left along a path (ditch on right) which eventually comes out onto a driveway at a footpath signpost. Go ahead to the road.

Turn right along **Orchard Road** (ignore a path to the left) to come to the lovely big green at **Burnham Green**. On the right of the crossroads is the village shop. Go straight ahead along **White Horse Lane** passing the pub of the same name.

Just before the speed de-limit sign, take the footpath on the right signed to **Coltsfoot Lane**. Go into a field by a garden fence and carry on ahead between undulating fields. Through a tree-lined boundary go down into the next field and carry on along the same line, passing a stand of trees on the right, to come out through a hedgerow onto **Coltsfoot Lane**.

↰ (6)

Turn right along this beautiful tree-lined lane, passing a farm and converted barns on the left and a footpath off to the right, to reach the hamlet of **Bull's Green**. The atmospheric **Horns pub** is to the left. Turn right to the road junction. Ignoring the road to Burnham Green to the right, continue along the **Bramfield Road**, passing **Moat Farm**, **Clibbon's Cottage**, and **Clibbon's House**. Further down the road is a post marking the grave of the notorious 18th century robber Walter Clibborn.

↰ (7)

A few yards past these properties, turn left down a wide, signed track (with limited parking). Pass a water tower on the right; then, at a junction of tracks, turn right alongside woodland with views over to more woods. Ignore a broad track to the right at a marker post and keep on ahead. A bridleway goes left, but the walk continues into the wonderful mixed woodland of **Bramfield Woods**, with old boundary banks and ditches and evidence of coppiced hazel.

↰ (8)

At a signed crossing of tracks, with wooden bollards ahead, turn right through mixed woodland towards **Symond's Wood**, avoiding all side paths. Go gently downhill to a road. Cross and continue ahead down **Tewin Hill**, overhung with ancient woodland. A footpath is signed to Tewin Wood on the right, but the walk continues to a road junction. Ignoring the road to Datchworth on the right, bear left, then right, round the continuation of Tewin Hill.

*On the left, **Elizabethan Queen Hoo Hall,** an exquisite building of glowing red brick with stone mullions, was possibly used as a hunting lodge.*

The walk continues gently down the winding hill, through woodland at first , and then with more open views, particularly to **Bramfield Park Wood**, an old hunting wood, on the left. Pass Tewin Hill Farm and come to a T-junction in **Tewin**. Turn right for the **Plume of Feathers** pub and the car park or left to visit the **Rose & Crown** in **Lower Green**.

Place of Interest Nearby

Digswell, 3 miles to the east, is the home of the spectacular **Digswell Viaduct** (take your camera!).

12 Ardeley

One of the interesting monuments in the churchyard of St

Distance 4½ miles   **Terrain** Fairly level
Map OS Explorer 194 Hertford and Bishops Stortford (GR 309273)

How to get there

Ardeley is signed from the B1037, which runs between Stevenage and Cottered. **Parking**: In a lay-by opposite the village hall, or just round the corner in School Lane.

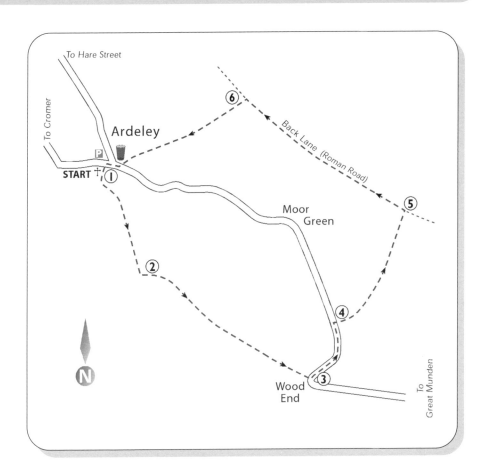

Introduction

Starting from the unusual hamlet of Ardeley, the walk passes through quintessential English farmland, a patchwork of woods and fields laced together by old green lanes. It takes a byway leading south through wooded farmland to reach the hamlet of Wood End, returning to Ardeley along a Roman road.

Refreshments

The 500-year-old **Jolly Waggoner's** in Ardeley is a lovely old-fashioned pub, with antique furniture and roaring fires in winter. Its cottage garden is pleasant for al fresco eating. Telephone: 01438 861350.

Drive and Stroll

THE WALK

The picturesque village hall and Arts and Crafts style thatched cottages on the green at Ardeley were designed in 1917 by F C Eden, but were the brainchild of the landowner, John Carter of Ardeley Bury, and Dr Eck, the vicar. Over the road the 13th century church of St Lawrence has a lovely Early English chancel, a fine piscina, and lancet windows in the north aisle. Twelve beautifully carved angels hold up the roof. There are interesting monuments and brasses of 1515, 1599, and 1885.

Turn right into **School Lane**, which borders the churchyard, and walk past the school and a crescent of houses to a broad gravel track passing through trees. The path wends its way downhill and meets a junction of farm tracks. Go straight on.

*To the right over the fields, there is a distant view of the towers of **Ardeley Bury**, a Tudor building restored in the Gothic style in about 1820.*

When the track forks, take the left-hand, wooded path. Keep ahead at another farm cross track.

At another signed crossing of paths, bear left along the main track (a tree-hung public byway to **Wood End**). The proliferation of rights of way and farm tracks can be confusing; so be sure to avoid cross tracks and keep ahead on the main path. There are now open views over fields as the path curves gently. The track comes to a marker post on the right at a complicated junction of five paths. Keep ahead along this byway. Soon there is another marker post, this time on the left. Continue ahead; then, ignoring a signed footpath to the left, keep on past a bungalow to a signpost at a cross track indicating Wood End ahead. Pass **Lite's Manor**; at the 30 mph sign, walk ahead onto a road, passing **Lite's Farm** and some attractive houses and cottages, to reach a road junction. (Note the Victorian post box in the flint wall.)

Turn left, signed to **Ardeley** and Cromer, passing a converted chapel. As the road bends to the left, ignore the footpath to a house called **Leycroft** on the right, and then a footpath to the left, and continue a little way to a another footpath signpost pointing right.

Turn right here. The path should go slightly to the left across the field, towards a large oak in the hedge. If it is not clear through the crop, walk along the edge of the field to the end of the hedgerow on the right, where the other footpath comes in; then walk ahead along the edge of a ditch on the left, past two mature trees, to an unmarked post at a footbridge. Cross the bridge and go left along a broad farm track to a bend at a footbridge in the hedge (route of the original path). Follow the farm track round, past a bricked-up cottage. Just beyond go through a kissing gate and bear right to walk in the same direction as before through a meadow with old trees. Go through a second kissing gate and along a causeway to a small gate. The lovely pool on the left, just off the old drove road, is **Wateringplace Green**, where stock was rested and watered. Cross a small section of meadow to another kissing gate to emerge onto a farm track.

When the farm track bears sharply right, go ahead through a gap in the hedgerow to a post on **Back Lane**, a Roman road. Turn left along this tree-hung track. Go over a little stream on a bridge by a ford, ignoring the paths to right and left. Continue for some distance, passing two paths to the left.

Cross a stile (marked with an arrow) to the left. Go a short distance over a field to another stile. Having negotiated this, bear right round the end of a manège and barns, to cross a stile in a fence. Bear left across the corner of the field (house over on left) and cross a stile by a fringe of lime trees. Go over the next little field to a metal signpost on a farm track. It indicates the direction to Ardeley, half-left along the edge of a field. Make for poplar trees and houses over the fields. Cross into the next field and follow the path through it. Cross into a further field, and, in a direct line with the church, follow the footpath through it. Go through a kissing gate at the end of the field and into a meadow by a farmyard. Cross this. Go through a wide farm gate into a stableyard and then through another big gate onto the drive of a cottage (the **Old Bell**). Go the short distance to the road near the **Jolly Waggoner's** pub. Turn right along the road to return to **School Lane**.

Place of Interest Nearby

Benington Lordship Gardens, near Stevenage, are set around the ruins of a Norman castle. Telephone: 08701 261709.

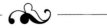

13 Whitwell and St Paul's Walden

St Paul's Walden Bury, home of the Bowes-Lyon family

Distance 3 miles   **Terrain** Hilly
Map OS Explorer 193 Luton and Stevenage (GR 193223)

How to get there

Not long after passing the Royal Oak pub on the B656, Hitchin to Codicote road, turn right onto the B651, signed to Whitwell. After 2 miles take a right turn just before the Strathmore Arms pub in the hamlet of St Paul's Walden to All Saints' church. **Parking**: In the car park outside the church or just across the lane from the church.

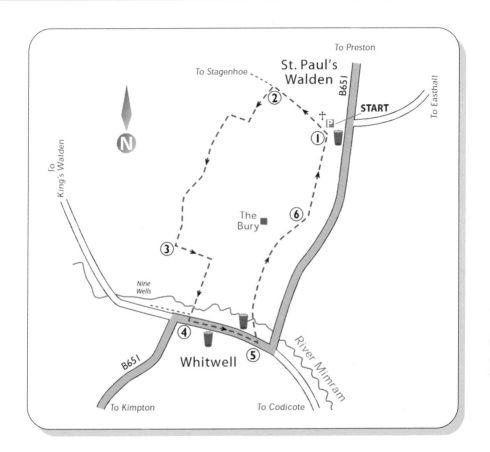

Introduction

This short walk is packed full of interest. It begins in the hamlet of St Paul's Walden and makes its way downhill towards Whitwell, in the valley of the river Mimram, passing through beautiful old woodland. It emerges onto the meadows of Bury Farm, with good views over the valley, before plunging into the shade of an old track to cross the river and enter Whitwell. The walk then ascends along the route of the Hertfordshire Way, cutting through the St Paul's Walden Bury estate with views of the listed garden surrounding the great house.

Refreshments

The Maiden's Head is a pleasant local in Whitwell, serving pub food. There are tables in the hilly garden behind. Telephone: 01438 871392.

Drive and Stroll

THE WALK

With your back to the Victorian postbox in the church wall, turn right along the small approach lane bounded by hedges and trees, ignoring another lane leading right.

Turn left (signpost) into a field, where a narrow path on the right leads straight ahead through a fringe of trees. Before long the track continues into lovely woodland. Follow the bends of the path, passing the remnants of old ponds and boundary banks and ditches as it goes downhill. Eventually the track emerges through a kissing gate into a meadow. Continue downhill, walking along the leafy right-hand boundary of a field overlooking the Mimram valley and Whitwell. Go through another kissing gate into a second field and continue, soon following the boundary as it curves left. At the boundary of a third field, bear right to another kissing gate. Go through this and continue straight on; then go down into a dip.

At the next hedgerow, turn left along it to traverse the slope. After a fairly short distance, bear right down steps to another kissing gate. Through this, bear left, and then almost immediately turn right at a cross track. This is a broad shady hollow way, lined with mixed trees and holly. Pass mellow brick **Water Hall Farm** on the left where the lane becomes metalled. Cross a brick bridge over the **Mimram**, passing pretty cottages to come out onto **Whitwell High Street**.

(To look at the watercress beds at **Nine Wells**, where watercress has been grown since the 18th century, turn right for a third of a mile.)

Turn left along the **High Street.** Pass the shop and post office, and then the **Maiden's Head** pub on the other side of the road.

*Note the names of the old houses and cottages, often recalling village activities of the past, such as the straw plaiting school: a pretty white timbered cottage on the right is called The Old Village Hall. **The Bull** pub, with its garden overlooking the watermeadows of the river Mimram, is opposite (telephone: 01438 871254).*

Ignore footpaths off to the right.

Turn left at a footpath signpost next to the red brick **Mill House**, bearing left through the yard, and go over a stile into a water meadow with traces of the former millstream on the left. Cross the meadow and go over a humpy concrete bridge, crossing stiles and going over a farm track to a stile ahead. Cross it and walk beside fencing on the left. (The meadows are likely to be divided up by electric fencing.) Go through a metal kissing gate at a field boundary and bear slightly right before continuing. Cross over a metal sheep hurdle into the next field and walk alongside a fence on the right to another hurdle.

*There are good views of **St Paul's Walden Bury**, the home of the Bowes Lyon family, where the late Queen Mother spent her childhood. Part of the house was built by James Paine in 1767, with the front possibly by Adam.*

Go through a metal kissing gate onto the drive. Bear right, ignoring a track on the right going down to the road and also a footpath going right. A magnificent avenue of limes forges its way down the hill here. Follow the curves of the drive.

There are glimpses on the left of the 18th century garden laid out by Edward Gilbert, with its lake, ponds,

temples, and statues, and of the old walled garden down on the right.

At a grassy triangle where the main drive bears right, the walk goes ahead along a lesser broad track, passing a neo-Gothic cottage. Continue uphill between lovely trees, with glimpses on the left of statuary and an octagonal summerhouse in the Bury grounds, and a plantation of unusual mixed trees on the right. **St Paul's Walden** church comes into view at the top of the track, where a footpath signpost points back to the village.

*The 12th century church of **All Saints** has a lavish chancel created in 1727 by Edward Gilbert, then the owner of the Bury; his memorial stone is in the chancel floor. A wall tablet commemorates the baptism here of the late Queen Mother.*

*In the village, the **Strathmore Arms**, belonging to the St Paul's Walden estate, does Sunday breakfast with newspapers. Telephone: 01438 871654.*

Place of Interest Nearby

Knebworth House is 5½ miles to the east. This stately home has formal gardens and parkland, and also an adventure playground with dinosaur trail. Telephone: 01438 812661.

14 Hexton

The Raven was built in 1913 to match the estate houses

Distance 3 miles   **Terrain** Mainly flat
Map OS Explorer 193 Luton and Stevenage (GR 106307)

How to get there

From the centre of Hitchin follow the signs to the A505, Luton road. Branch right at a mini roundabout along the B655 signed to Barton-le-Clay. Hexton is signed right off this road, before reaching Barton-le-Clay. **Parking**: In the main street, near the Raven pub.

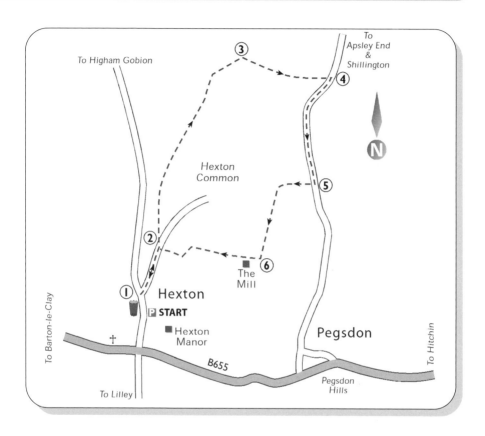

Introduction

In the north-west of the county, a finger of Hertfordshire, dominated by outcrops of the Chiltern Hills, sticks up into the underbelly of Bedfordshire, The evidence of settlement at Hexton, with its favoured position just off the Icknield Way, near the Iron Age hill fort of Ravensburgh Castle, goes back long before Domesday Book, when there were about 35 households. The manor of Hexton had passed from Danish hands to the Abbot of St Albans, but following the Reformation a succession of farsighted lords (and ladies) of the manor stamped their mark on the manor and the village. Caroline de Latour lived at Hexton Manor for 70 years. She employed most of the villagers on the farm and estate, enlarging the house and laying out pleasure gardens, erecting a village pump, renovating the church and creating a village school. After her death in 1869, the estate fell into disrepair until George Hodgson took over at the turn of the century, and restored the

Drive and Stroll

manor, and rebuilt the village as a model estate. The walk passes through flat farmland and woodland dominated by sweeping views of the Pegsdon, Hexton and Barton hills sheltering the settlements below. On the return to Hexton, there are glimpses of Hexton Manor and its parkland.

Refreshments

The Raven Inn was built in 1913 to match the estate houses. The pub provides excellent food and beer, and has a children's play area and a heated patio as well as a garden. Telephone: 01582 881209.

THE WALK

From **The Raven**, turn left along the main street, crossing the turning to Higham Gobion. Continue along **Common Lane** (which eventually becomes a track that peters out at Hexton Common), past cottages and farmhouses, many of them in Arts and Crafts style.

Where **Common Lane** bears right, take the footpath ahead, signed through a field. The path comes to a marker post at a plantation of mixed trees and shrubs; continue ahead here along a grassy headland bordering the plantation. Follow the direction of the next marker post, ahead through the middle of a field. (Here there are views towards the church at **Higham Gobion** on the hillside on the left.) The path skirts a copse on the right and carries on ahead (marker post), in line with **Shillington church** on a hillock ahead. This is the area of **Hexton Common**. Ignore a farm cross-track and go straight on alongside a ditch. Where the track bears left, keep ahead over a wooden footbridge (arrow-marked) and go straight across a field towards a hedgerow. A path goes off left in the middle of the field, but keep ahead to a bridge with a marker post.

Cross the bridge and turn right alongside a hedge and ditch or stream. (Now Shillington church appears slightly more to the left.) At a field boundary at the corner, a Bedfordshire yellow marker post shows a junction of paths. Go through the hedgerow here and straight on across a field towards a wood. (There are now lovely views of the **Pegsdon Hills**, far over on the right.) At the end of this field a marker post points ahead into another field, along a broad track beside a wood on the left. The wood ends, and there are open fields through the hedgerow on the left. Where the wide grassy track bears right, the walk continues ahead along a narrow footpath through old woodland, which hides a moat. Go through a metal gate into a field near farm buildings and bear right along a raised causeway to a kissing gate in the fence. Go through and bear left down the drive of **Apsley Bury Farm** to come out through wooden gates onto a road at a footpath signpost.

 4

Turn right along the road, passing the gates of **Shillington Manor** (another moated site) on the left and a cottage on the right. Follow the bends of this small road for some distance, enjoying the panorama of hills ahead. Pass a house and then the entrance to **Kettledean Farm.**

 5

Not long after this, turn right along a bridleway (signed) through the middle of a field. Before long the track turns left alongside a hedge on the left, making for trees.

 6

Where the bridleway comes out onto a track at a corner, turn right. Bear right to a mill where the lane becomes metalled (**Mill Lane**).

*Through the odd gap in the tall hedge on the left, you can see glimpses of **Hexton Manor** and its parkland trees. The present house was built in 1770, replacing an earlier one.*

Follow the bends of the lane, eventually passing a sewage works on the left, to reach a T-junction with **Common Lane**. Turn left here, pass the footpath taken on the outward journey, and retrace your steps along the street to the **Raven pub**.

***St Faith's church**, with its ruined tower, stands isolated from the main village on the Barton Road; though heavily restored, it dates back to the 12th century.*

Place of Interest Nearby

Just 5 miles north of Hexton, near Silsoe, is **Wrest Park** (English Heritage), a magnificent early 18th century garden, with canals and pavilions. Telephone: 01525 860152.

15 Lilley

There are many estate cottages in Lilley

Distance 4½ miles   **Terrain** Along well-defined tracks
Map OS Explorer 193 Luton and Stevenage (GR 118265)

How to get there

Lilley is signed off the A505, two thirds of the way between Hitchin and Luton. **Parking**: Kerbside outside the Lilley Arms or at Treasures Grove, reached by carrying on through Lilley and turning right for a short distance to the next road junction on the Icknield Way.

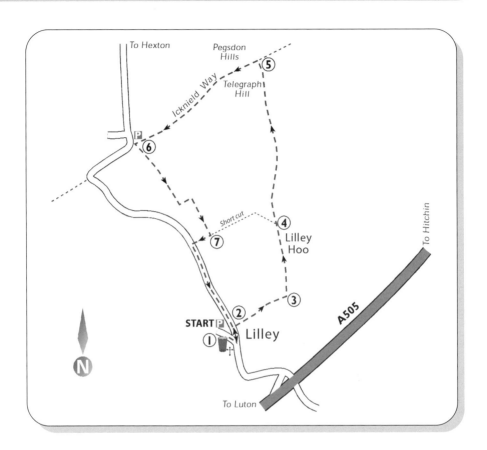

Introduction

Rupert Brooke, who often walked the Icknield Way here while studying at Cambridge, wrote of 'the Roman Road to Wendover, by Tring and Lilley Hoo', which forms part of this varied and hilly walk. It starts in the estate village of Lilley, on the border of Bedfordshire, and climbs up onto Lilley Hoo, once a sheep-grazed downland plateau and then a racecourse. At the northern end is Telegraph Hill. From here the route is along prehistoric Icknield Way, which passes along a ridge of the Chilterns. Lining the route is a wealth of earthworks and other ancient sites, some connected with Neolithic man, others with the Saxons, Vikings, or Romans. The return to Lilley follows part of the John Bunyan Trail. Bunyan reputedly preached in the cellar of a 17th century cottage still in existence in Lilley, and several houses in the village were registered for worship by Dissenters.

Drive and Stroll

Refreshments

The Lilley Arms, a 300-year-old former coaching inn, once known as the Sowerby Arms, welcomes walkers, cyclists, and riders (a hitching post and cycle racks are provided). It provides real ales and home cooked food. There is a large garden, and accommodation is available. Telephone: 01462 768371.

THE WALK

From the pub return to the main road.

Just down the road to the right, is the church of St Peter, rebuilt in 1870, which has a Norman arch in the chancel.

Turn left along **East Street**, passing on the left a pair of estate cottages with pointed gables and the crest of a lion rampant belonging to Thomas Dowcra, who owned the manor in the 16th century.

Soon take a signed bridleway to the right up **The Baulk**, a broad stony lane, passing a few houses. Bear slightly left at a cottage and follow the track as it narrows downhill. At a crossing of signed paths, continue ahead, going uphill through high hedges to a signpost.

Go left towards **Telegraph Hill**. Go through a boundary and walk along a broad track on the left-hand side of a field, at first along the edge of woodland. (There are excellent views over the countryside through gaps in the hedge when the wood ends.) Ignore a bridleway which goes through the field on the right and soon come to a signpost.

(The branch straight on, signed **Lilley** via **Kingshill Lane**, provides a SHORT CUT.)

Turn right here to cross the fairly narrow field to another signpost by woodland. Ignoring the path signed right to Hollybush Hill, turn left to **Telegraph Hill**, along a broad stony track alongside woodland. This is the tableland of **Lilley Hoo**, once the site of a racecourse often patronized by the Prince Regent, later George IV. Ignore a bridleway to the right and continue ahead, following the signed track to Telegraph Hill through the middle of fields. Go under power lines. Ignoring a permissive path going left, keep ahead, following the gentle bends of the path alongside a hedge and passing a bridleway to the right. After leaving the hedge, continue towards trees, ignoring a track on the left. A right-hand track goes to Little Offley, but continue through woodland to an information board about Telegraph Hill, a Herts and Middlesex Wildlife Trust Nature Reserve valued for its archaeological and wildlife interest. Its name comes from a wooden telegraph station built in 1808 to link London's Admiralty to Great Yarmouth.

 5

At a Chiltern Way and Icknield Way signpost turn left onto **Icknield Way**. (Just beyond is a broader track, where a signpost gives information about the Pegsdon Hills, a nature reserve with archaeological sites.) Go along the small track following the course of this prehistoric route linking Wiltshire with East Anglia, which in the past was a series of roughly parallel tracks, possibly forged through woodland by herdsmen. Ignore all paths off, and continue downhill through a variety of woodland. Eventually the track comes out into the open and has wide flowery verges. Continue to a signpost near Treasures Grove car park.

 6

Leave the **Icknield Way** here and go left at a marker post up a broad farm track, now part of the **John Bunyan** Trail. There are farm buildings on the right as the path goes under power lines. Pass through open fields, and, ignoring a farm track to the right, go straight on alongside woodland on the right. A footpath is signed right, but this walk bears left, then right, and then passes through open fields, eventually reaching a permissive path to the left. Where the John Bunyan Trail goes right at an arrow marker, go straight on up the edge of a field to a marker post where **Kingshill Lane** (SHORT CUT) goes uphill between hedges to the left.

 7

Turn right here to go through fields towards the houses of **Lilley** and the main street. Walk left along the pavement through the village, passing **Ward's Farm**, scattered houses (some with the lion rampant), and a pond on the right. Ignoring a footpath signed to the right just before the left turn up The Baulk taken at the start of the walk, continue back to the pub.

Place of Interest Nearby

Four miles to the east of Lilley are **Galley Hill** and **Warden Hill**, which are nature reserves on an outcrop of the Chilterns.

16 Aspenden

Charles Lamb's Cottage at Button Snap, near

Distance 6 miles   **Terrain** Mostly farm tracks
Map OS Explorer 194 Hertford and Bishops Stortford (GR 353283)

How to get there

Leave the A10 at the Buntingford roundabout (where the A507 goes off to Baldock). Follow the signs into Buntingford to reach a T-junction with High Street. Turn right here and look for signs to Aspenden and Westmill on the right before leaving the town. Turn right and follow the road round under the A10 to reach Aspenden and its pleasant green. Bear right at the next road junction to the main street. **Parking**: Along the far (western) end of the main street or near the church; please park with consideration.

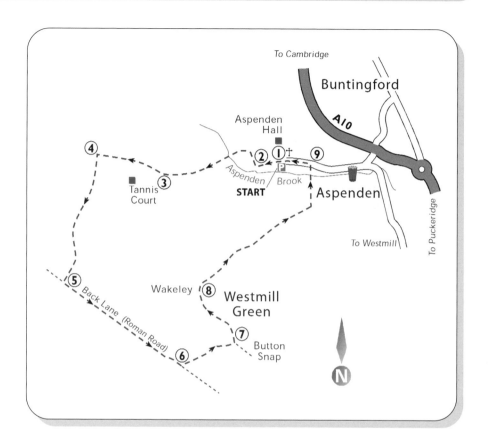

Introduction

It is perhaps surprising that, in the busy and built-up county of Hertfordshire, you can walk for six miles through farm and meadowland in total tranquility. Most of the tracks are ancient, one of them Roman, and you can almost imagine yourself to be back in the Dark Ages if you ignore the arable fields beyond the fringes of trees. The walk passes near moated Tannis Court before taking a track bordering the Old Bourne, passing Berkesdongreen Spring, which probably was once a watering place for drove animals. After a stretch on Roman Back Lane, a bridleway takes the walk north-east, out onto an isolated lane near the pretty thatched cottage of Buttonsnap, which once belonged to Charles Lamb. Another old track passes the site of the deserted village of Wakeley before heading downhill back to Aspenden.

Drive and Stroll

Refreshments

The Fox inn, situated in the long main street of Aspenden, has a lovely sheltered garden, and the menu is interesting and reasonably priced. It is closed at lunchtime on Tuesday and open for drinks only on Tuesday evenings. Telephone: 01763 271886.

THE WALK

Near the church is a footpath sign to **Tannis Court**. Walk ahead along the stony track with trees on the left.

At a marker post at a parting of the ways, carry on along the main right-hand track to a signpost. Avoid the grassy track ahead and go left along the gravelly track, which continues for about a mile, with wide views over farmland. Eventually the barns of **Tannis Court** come into view.

At a 'private' notice bear right (arrow marker) through the hedge into a field. Turn left (signed) along the edge of the field beside a hedgerow. Look out for and cross a footbridge on the left. Turn right (arrow marker), with a hedgerow now on the right. Go through by fence posts to another arrow marker, which points left, but there is a path left through the crops ahead. Go through into the next field and continue with the hedge on the right. Ignoring an arrow marker which points slightly left, across the corner of a field, bear right through a hedge. Go over a footbridge to the right to reach the track of the **Old Bourne**.

Turn left along this broad track at the edge of a field. By **Berkesdongreen Spring**, hidden by trees, a sign near a metal gate marks several paths. Go through a gap between the metal gate and wooden fencing (red arrow). Turn left along this shady hedged track. At a T-junction of farm tracks with a footpath marker to the left, turn right along a shady track, almost a causeway, with ditches on both sides.

At a signpost onto **Back Lane**, near a ford, turn left along the wide shady track. Pass a lane to Wood End going off right at a farm track crossing. A metal gate bars the track where a second track goes off to the right. Pass to one side of the gate and continue ahead.

Look for an unmarked but obvious track leading left off **Back Lane**, through the hedgerow by a large ash tree. Walk along the edge of a field with a hedgerow on the right. At the end of the field carry straight on through a copse of young trees to a gate. Go through a gap by it and turn right along the edge of the field here. When the hedge veers off to the right, continue ahead across the corner of this small field to reach a gate with a bridleway signpost.

The route goes to the left here, along a small road.

However, it is worth making a short detour to the right to see **Buttonsnap**, *which once belonged to Charles Lamb. Set into the verge is his bust or medallion, which was presented to the Charles Lamb Society by the Westminster Bank when it was removed from their premises in Chancery Lane in 1965.*

Returning to the left along the lane, continue to the grassy area of **Westmill Green** on the right.

Continue along a concrete farm road leading to **Wakeley Farm**, passing a pond on the left. Where the farm road swings left (signpost), turn right along a broad bridleway through a metal gate. In a wooded area to the left is the site of the deserted medieval village of **Wakeley** and a spring. Leaving the wooded area, the track continues through fields. The track becomes more grassy and tree hung as it goes gently downhill. Where the wide track runs into a field, go ahead along a narrow grassy path to the right of it, which goes downhill through an edging of trees and bushes with a deep ditch on the left. It bears left at a farm gate. At an arrow-marked cross track, continue, going steeply downhill between high banks to emerge onto the main street of Aspenden.

Turn right to visit the **Fox** or left towards medieval St Mary's church and parking place.

Place of Interest Nearby

Buntingford, just to the north of Aspenden, has a wealth of character and many interesting old buildings to see, including the **Seth Ward** almshouses in the High Street, built in 1684.

17 | Furneux Pelham

A peaceful lane through Furneux Pelham

Distance 5 miles   **Terrain** Undulating
Map OS Explorer 194 Hertford and Bishops Stortford (GR 432279)

How to get there

From Buntingford take the B1038 to Hare Street. Turn right onto the B1368 and then, almost at the end of the village, turn left along a small lane signed to Little Hormead and Furneux Pelham. Take the next right turn in Little Hormead and follow the bends of the lane into Furneux Pelham. **Parking**: In the main street near the church or at Patmore Heath Nature Reserve.

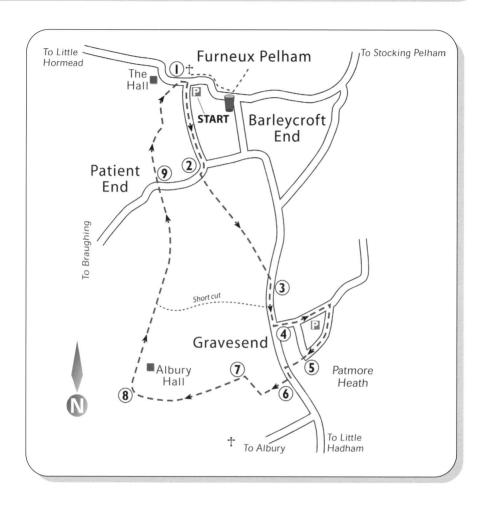

Introduction

The countryside around Furneux Pelham, near Hertfordshire's border with Essex, is a patchwork of woods and fields set in prettily undulating land curving down to the little river Ash. The walk starts along an elevated lane offering good views down into the valley. Field paths take the walker to the pretty hamlet of Gravesend and Patmore Heath Nature Reserve. From here the route descends into the valley and crosses the river Ash before entering the beautiful woods and meadows of the Albury estate on the way back to the village. There is a short extension through the village to the Brewery Tap pub.

Drive and Stroll

Refreshments

Beer used to be brewed at Rayment's Brewery in Furneux Pelham until the late 20th century. The lovely listed brewery buildings are now dwellings, but the **Brewery Tap** opposite, now a Greene King pub, still offers a special pint and welcome food, including international dishes as well as British pub favourites. Telephone: 01279 777280.

THE WALK

Coming out of the churchyard, turn right and then almost immediately left along **The Causeway**, passing a former pub, **The Star**, on the right. The lane leaves the village and continues to a road junction just beyond thatched **Pheasant Hall**.

Turn right for a short distance (signed to **Braughing**); then turn left down a broad field path at a metal signpost. Go gently downhill to cross a footbridge over the little **river Ash**; then, having crossed a farm track, walk half-right up through a field towards trees and a signpost on the skyline.

Turn right along the road, ignoring a footpath on the left, and walk into the hamlet of **Gravesend**.

(A signed path to the right offers a SHORT CUT back to Furneux Pelham.)

Continue past pretty cottages and turn left up a lane signed to **Patmore Heath**. (Sadly the old **Catherine Wheel** pub on the corner burnt down.) A lane bears right, along the edge of Patmore Heath (Herts and Middlesex Wildlife Trust), a nature reserve which is scarce example of a grass heath habitat with ponds. (A board further into the reserve gives a full explanation.) Either follow the lane ahead, bearing right alongside the heath, then continue bearing right, or follow paths through the reserve to reach the lane on the other side. Lanes form a triangle around the heath, with cottages sprinkled along its edge.

Make for the southern corner and look for **Hitch Lane Cottage** on the left. Go ahead through trees next to the cottage and pass buildings. Then take a right fork alongside a field, heading towards cottages. Pass through metal barriers to the road. Turn left along **High Hall Road**.

Soon, opposite **High Hall**, turn right down a wide gravelly bridleway, passing farm buildings. At the end of some barns continue straight on. Go downhill, crossing a bridge over the **river Ash** and ignoring the footpath to the left. Continue ahead at the arrow markers. Shortly, at a field boundary, turn right.

At **Filbert Copse**, where a grassy track goes ahead, turn left beside the copse along a broad grassy track with the copse on the right and a view of the spire of Albury church on the left. This is part of the **Harcamlow Way**. Go over an arrow-marked cross path by a wood, slipping slightly to the right to continue on the same line as before, first through woodland and then with a field on the right. The path comes out through beautiful oak trees onto a lane. Bear right here. Continue to a marker post where a path forks right but keep ahead along the metalled lane through wooded farmland. Look for a signpost at the end of woodland on the right.

The bridleway goes ahead, but the walk follows the footpath through a metal kissing gate to the right through trees. Soon the path comes out at a signpost onto a grassy area with houses opposite. Cross the grass to another signpost, and go straight ahead along a lane between

The Brewery Tap at Furneux Pelham

farm buildings. **Albury Hall** is hidden in trees. Where the lane bends to the left (marker post) near a driveway on the right, the walk carries straight on along a gravelly track with a pond on the right. Leave the track where a footpath swings right and go straight ahead onto a wide field path, heading towards **Furneux Pelham** church. (This is now the **Hertfordshire Way**.) At the brow of the hill the path swings left for a short distance to a signpost, and then right again, following the same line as before. Go gently downhill between two fields with good views. At another marker post, keep ahead, ignoring a footpath to the right. Cross an arrow-marked bridge over a ditch and carry on up the middle of a field towards pretty cottages and an old redbrick farmhouse (**Patient End Farm**). Keep alongside a hedge to reach the road at Patient End (signpost).

Drive and Stroll

🔖 ⑨

Turn left along the lane for a very short distance; then go right at a signpost along a driveway. Pass a pretty pargetted cottage and then the farmhouse. Where the bridleway goes left, go ahead along a signed footpath beside a barn conversion. Go over a stile and along the edge of a meadow. The footpath runs a little way in from the left-hand boundary and goes down to a marked stile in a fence. Cross the stile into the next field and bear slightly right across the middle of it. Go over another stile (arrow-marked) and go straight on, ignoring the alternative path half right.

*Ahead, there is a glimpse of the Dutch gables of **Furneux Pelham Hall**, built in the 17th century of red brick. This was the home of Catholic Lord Mounteagle, who betrayed the conspirators of the Gunpowder Plot.*

Carry on down the meadow to a stile and a little footbridge over a ditch (arrow-marked). Go ahead, but soon bear slightly to the right to reach and cross an arrow-marked stile in a fence. Go over a footbridge and pass between a pumping station and a cottage to reach the road. Turn left along **The Causeway** to the main road; then go a short way to the right to reach the church.

St Mary's church has a roof of colourful angels and some window glass by William Morris and Sir Edward Burne Jones.

Continue from the church for half a mile past scattered houses to reach **Barleycroft End**, where **The Brewery Tap** pub stands on a crossroads.

*Opposite are the converted buildings of **Rayment's Brewery**, with its maltings built in 1860 alongside a small tributary of the river Ash. The northern route of the river is along **Violets Lane** which runs along the bed of the river for a mile. When the river is high, a long stretch of the lane becomes a causeway along which people can paddle!*

Place of Interest Nearby

To the west of Saffron Walden is **Audley End House** (English Heritage). This is a magnificent house spanning several periods, with notable gardens including an organic walled Victorian kitchen garden. Telephone: 01799 522399 (information line), or 01799 510444 (Tourist Information Centre).

18 | Rushden

One of Rushden's many attractive cottages

Distance 3½ miles   **Terrain** Gentle hills
Map OS Explorer 194 Hertford and Bishops Stortford (GR 305317)

How to get there

Turn left off the A507 from Baldock to Buntingford at Cumberlow Green. Rushden is signed right, about a mile along this lane. **Parking**: At the car park in Church End, between the church and the village hall.

Drive and Stroll

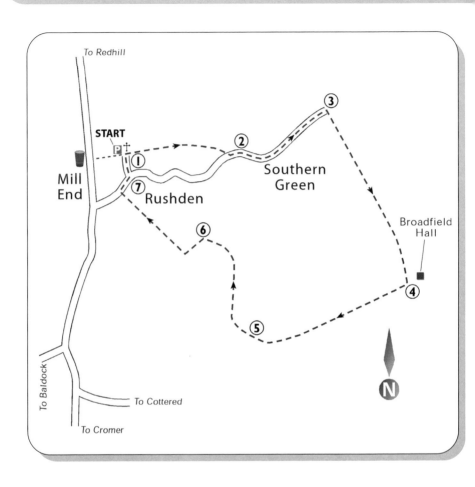

Introduction

Rushden is an idyllic small village of timbered or weatherboarded houses and cottages, with some plaster and flint for variation, set below the church of St Mary. It has several satellite hamlets, including Southern Green, Cumberlow Green, Shaw Green, and Offley Green, and some notable country houses such as Julians and Broadfield Hall. The river Beane rises near Rushden. This rural walk follows lovely field paths to the hamlet of Southern Green. A narrow hedged lane winds east to join a broad track leading to Broadfield Hall, where there are extensive views over the countryside. Wide tracks and small footpaths then take the walker through farmland back to Rushden.

Refreshments

The Moon and Stars, a pretty cottagey old pub at Mill End, is hung with cheerful flower baskets. It offers excellent beer and pub food. Telephone: 01763 288330

THE WALK

From the car park, go through a kissing gate with arrow markers into the churchyard and walk to the right, in front of **St Mary's church**, to an arrow-marked stile. Cross this, and go ahead across a meadow and through a kissing gate (arrow-marked) in a wooden fence. Walk alongside the hedge on the left, with a house over the field on the right.

Through a gap in the hedge, there is a view of Julians over the fields on the left. In part early Georgian, with a lovely garden, it was visited by the author Anthony Trollope, and in earlier times the manor was owned by the Flemish ambassador to Queen Elizabeth I.

Go through a kissing gate and onto a boardwalk, where a track crosses. Keep ahead (marker post) through a wooded area and then into a field, bearing half-left across it and leaving it along a narrow path between thatched cottages. Walk on into **Southern Green** (signpost).

Bear left and then right along a road, passing **Southern Green Farm** on the left. Follow the bends of this almost traffic-free lane for about half a mile.

At a signpost at a T-junction of lanes, turn right (signed to **Broadfield Lodge Farm**), ignoring the footpath off to the left. Walk along this small lane alongside a high hedge, passing a house and then Jubilee Cottage on the left. Go through a gate into a farmyard. Continue along the metalled track, going slightly uphill. Go through a gateway, passing a farmhouse on the left with woods behind, and continue past Hall Farm (painted white) and its red brick dovecote set back on the left. Ignore the first signed footpath to the right and continue a little way, passing the entrance to **Broadfield Hall**.

Turn right here, along a broad stony signed track which soon goes alongside a band of woodland on the left. A footpath goes left, but the walk continues downhill to a crossing of paths near a signpost, which directs the route straight uphill to another arrow marker.

Drive and Stroll

⤵ (5)

Ignoring the bridleway, take the footpath to the right and follow it round beside a hedge and wood on the left. At the end of the wood, where the field track turns left, an arrow marker points sharp right. Walk between fields alongside a hedge on the right. The hedge veers slightly off to the right, while the path continues towards a gap in the adjoining hedge. Go through and bear left to a signpost pointing straight ahead along a narrow path through woodland. Keep ahead past a mysterious pond on the left to another signpost and go downhill through old woodland to a footbridge. Cross this by a footpath marker and go gently uphill along the edge of a field.

⤵ (6)

Go through a wooded hedgerow into another field and turn left (marker post) to walk along the edge of a field. At a boundary, go through into the next field (signpost), and turn right along a field with a hedgerow on the right. Walk gently up and then downhill. Go through at a tree edged boundary into the next field and continue along the hedgerow and trees on the right. The

hedgerow thins out at the garden of thatched **Field Cottage**. Continue ahead, along tarmac, passing a converted barn. Ignore a crossing of footpaths and go along **Treacle Lane** past the pretty cottages of **Rushden**.

⤵

Turn right to **Church End** to go back to the car park and **St Mary's church**.

The church – built of rendered flint with a later, white brick chancel – has 500-year-old beams inside, with 15th century corbels carved with lively faces. The octagonal font is also 15th century, and there is a monument to the Flemish ambassador Meetkerkes, who lived at Julians.

To reach **The Moon and Stars** at **Mill End**, walk in the opposite direction to the church, going left through a gap in the car park hedge and downhill through a meadow with a variety of lovely mature trees. Cross a stile by a garden and continue to a footbridge which leads to the main road (signpost). The pub is across the road. Nearby is **Hammers**, once the old forge, which was visited by the Duke of Wellington.

Place of Interest Nearby

Letchworth is about 5 miles due east of Rushden, and there is much to see and do there, including the **Heritage Museum** where you can learn the story of the first garden city. Telephone: 01462 482710.

19 | Reed and Barkway

The cabinet at Fiddler's Green, Reed

Distance 4 or 5½ miles   **Terrain** Level
Map OS Explorer 194 Hertford and Bishops Stortford (GR 362357)

How to get there

Reed is signed left off the A10 from Royston to Buntingford. Drive along Blacksmith's Lane; then turn right into Church Lane to reach the church.
Parking: Near the church in Reed or at the village hall in Barkway.

Drive and Stroll

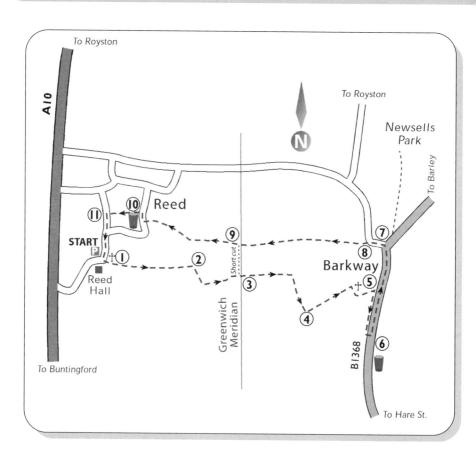

Introduction

The high land between Reed and Barkway, an eastern extension of the Chiltern Hills, is filled with history. Reed, built on a grid of small lanes, is the site of a Roman camp, and Roman silver was found in the 18th century in Rokey Wood, part of this walk. The sites of several moats and old fish ponds, as well as Periwinkle Hill, an ancient motte and bailey, are passed en route. Barkway, by contrast, had the makings of an important market town, and there are several old coaching inns with arched gateways which served this staging post on the route from London. Outside Barkway House is a milestone – one of fifteen between here and Cambridge – erected around 1725 by two Fellows of Trinity College, Cambridge. The walk can be varied in length by means of a shortcut or an extension from Barkway along a path to the atmospheric Newsells estate.

Refreshments

A popular choice for special eating, the **Cabinet** at Fiddler's Green has little old bars, a pleasant restaurant, and a large grassy garden. Telephone: 01763 848366.

THE WALK

Go through a kissing gate and walk ahead through the graveyard, with the **church of St Mary** on the left – the north doorway dates back to 1090. At the far end of the churchyard look for a gap in the hedge and go straight across a field towards trees. Cross a farm track and continue ahead through a fringe of trees; go over a little footbridge to a post (arrow-marked) at a crossing of paths. Go ahead up quite a steep bank into a field and continue across the middle towards a large clump of trees. (There are tall communications masts on the horizon.)

At a farm track by trees, where a marker post indicates a footpath to the left, our route continues ahead along the farm track, passing a warning sign for low flying aircraft. (This is part of the **Hertfordshire Way**. There are views over fields on the right to a windsock.) Bear right, following the track round woodland on the left. At the end of the woodland, at an arrow marker, go left through the hedgerow to another arrow marker. Bear right along the edge of the field to a farm track (arrow marker), and bear left along the track, which is good and wide, passing between woodland and open fields. The track kinks round the end of woodland hiding a moat, before resuming the same direction, and then swinging left alongside Rokey Wood.

(To the left is a permissive route which offers a SHORT CUT back to **Reed**. The line of the Greenwich Meridian crosses the main path near here.)

Continue ahead along a wide grassy track (marker post) beside the wood. Eventually the path narrows where the wood ends and passes between two lines of greenery for a short distance before coming out into the open and bearing gently to the right, with views of **Barkway** and its church tower ahead. At a marker post, avoid the footpath going left and carry on along the main bridleway, which continues to curve right alongside a hedge and ditch. After some distance the grassy track becomes gravelly and goes on between fences to a metal signpost indicating a byway to Strawberry Grove to the right and a footpath straight on into a field.

Drive and Stroll

Go left, along a broad track which soon becomes metalled and passes manicured gardens and a lovely pond to reach the wall of Barkway churchyard.

*The tower of **St Mary Magdalene church** was rebuilt in 1861 and adorned with pinnacles. The chancel dates from the 13th century. There is some late 15th century stained glass, and, notable among several monuments, is one by Rysbrack to Rear-Admiral Sir John Jennings MP, who died in 1743.*

Near the church stands Jacobean Manor Farm and its old barns.

Bear right, following the church wall as it curves round to the lychgate, where a raised causeway leads to the road, passing an old brick-walled cart pond and weatherboarded cottages.

Turn right to explore the southern end of Barkway's beautiful **High Street**.

*Where the road widens near the village pond and the sign opposite **The Limes** is the site of the old market. A lovely range of houses and cottages, some dating to the 16th or 17th century, leads to the chunky red brick **Stalleybrass Almshouses** of 1909. Over the road*

*is the little yellow brick bathhouse built by the Hon. Mrs Vernon Harcourt in 1867. Further on from this is a curve of cottages including **Berg Cottage** (National Trust), dated 1687.*

Walk back on the other side of the road, crossing **Burr's Lane**.

*Some modern houses are built with an arch to echo the old coaching inns. Facing Church Lane are two old coaching inns with archways leading to stabling behind; then there is an interesting mix of old houses and cottages, including **Red House**, an early Georgian building with a lovely carved door surround. Near the junction with **Royston Road** are **Half Moon Cottage** of around 1600, and a pretty timbered cottage of about 1500.*

*The village hall car park is just a short way along **Cambridge Road** (B1368) and the **Tally Ho** pub (telephone: 01763 848389), which serves good beers and pub food, is some distance further.*

Just before the **village hall** is a footpath signpost pointing the way to **Newsells** (¾ mile), once an almost deserted hamlet but now restored. This route can be taken as an extension to the walk, returning the same way to continue the main walk at point 8.

8

Turn left off the **High Street** and walk a short way along **Royston Road**. Where the road bends to the right, cross and go ahead along a broad track, ignoring a footpath signed to the left. Carry on along this byway through farmland to reach a marker post at the end of hedging. Where a footpath goes to the right, carry straight on, going gently uphill between fields. Then pass **Rokey Wood** on the left, with **Periwinkle Hill** on the right.

 9

At the end of the wood (where the SHORT CUT (point 2) rejoins the main route), carry on ahead between fields and parcels of woodland. Where the farm track swings right, go straight ahead at an arrow marker post. Ignoring a footpath to the right, keep straight on to a marker post at a junction of tracks. Continue straight on, soon going through a strip of woodland with old coppiced trees. Pass

between a pumping station and a cottage, to walk to the right onto a lane in **Reed** at a signpost. Go to the right along **High Street**, ignoring the lane called **Driftway**, to reach **The Cabinet** pub.

 10

Just after passing the pond in the pub garden, turn left through a kissing gate (signed) and go across a meadow, skirting some hedging and an old pond, to an arrow-marked gateway. (Houses and cottages are scattered around this central area of meadows.) Go through the gateway and take the path ahead, ignoring one to the right and passing a garden hedge, to a wooden kissing gate onto a lane.

 11

Turn left opposite the cricket field. Pass another pond and then the brick school and chapel of 1842, where Driftway goes left. Return to the church along the wide verges of tree-hung **Church Lane**, passing a footpath to the right.

Places of Interest Nearby

Just 3 miles north of Reed is the town of Royston where **Royston Cave** is open to the public on certain days during the year. It contains medieval carvings possibly associated with the Knights Templar. Telephone: 01763 245484. Also in Royston is the **museum** with exhibits on local history and archaeology. Telephone: 01763 242587.

20 Ashwell

High Street, Ashwell, showing the pargetted Guild

Distance 2 miles   **Terrain** Some hills
Map OS Explorer 193 Luton and Stevenage (GR 270398)

How to get there

Ashwell is signed off the A505 between Baldock and Royston. **Parking**: In the High Street by the railings of the springs, just beyond the Three Tuns. In dry weather cars can be parked at the end of the recreation ground (public toilets).

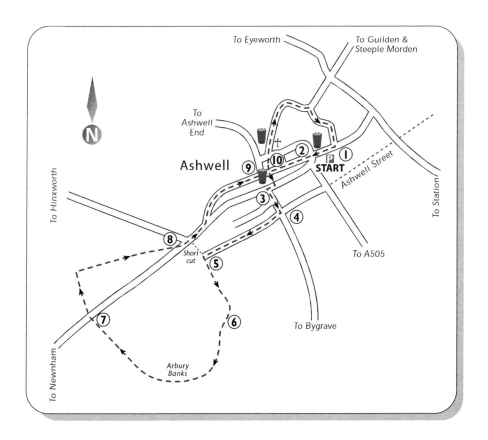

Introduction

Ashwell, in the north of the county, was an early settlement along pre-historic Icknield Way (here Ashwell Street), and was famous for its clear waters flowing from seven springs in a basin below the chalk escarpment, forming the river Rhee, a tributary of the Cam. At the time of *Domesday*, Ashwell was one of the wealthiest and most important market towns in Hertfordshire (the timbered Tudor Museum was probably formerly a market house), and evidence of its wealth can be seen in the many large early farm and manor houses, its numerous former ale houses, and the size of its beautiful 14th century church. The walk explores the village before making for historic Ashwell Street and the Iron Age hill fort of Arbury Banks, with spectacular views over huge sweeping fields under immense skies. From every point on the route can be seen the watchful church spire dominating the scene for miles around.

Drive and Stroll

Refreshments

The Rose and Crown, situated in High Street, dates back to the early 16th century. It offers good beers and excellent food, with an emphasis on fish. Telephone: 01462 742420. The 18th century **Three Tuns Hotel** near the Springs is a welcoming hostelry with a good menu and a large garden. Telephone: 01462 742107.

THE WALK

The walk begins at the springs (an SSSI, protecting the rare Ice Age flatworms *Crenobia alpina* and *Polycelis felina*). From the springs, walk to the right along the High Street, passing the Georgian **Three Tuns Hotel** on the right, with red brick **Jessamine House** (once a farm) opposite. This imposing house dates back to the 16th century with 18th century embellishments. Further on is the post office, with **Kingsland Way** going up the hill just beyond.

Continue over the junction with **Hodwell.**

A short detour to the right down Hodwell to where the lane bends to the left is the early 19th century village lock-up, made of clunch blocks from a demolished chantry chapel on the north side of the church.

On returning to the route of the walk, pass timbered **Foresters' Cottages** on the right, originally a 14th century hall house that was saved from demolition in 1959. Further on, on the right, is **Vine Cottage** (17th century in origin), opposite yellow brick **Whitby Farm**. On the corner of **Church Lane** is **Plait Hall**, an early timber-framed building which was once a straw-plaiting school supplying the hat trade in Luton. Cross over Church Lane, passing the heavily pargetted Guild House of 1681 – which is attached to the late 15th century **Guildhall of St John**, now divided into cottages – and a baker's shop. Next door, **The Adelong** was built in the Victorian period from profits from the Australian goldfields. Opposite is an ancient building called **Chippings** (now a hairdressers'), from the Old English word for a market or market place. Turn left up the signed footpath which goes through the grounds of the jettied 16th century **Rose and Crown** to emerge over a stile onto **Silver Street**, opposite the Victorian school (1878) with its fine bell tower. Turn right for a short distance to the road junction.

Turn left up **Bear Lane.** Continue over **Dixies Close** (named after the farm which originally occupied this land), up steps on the right, and past cottages to reach **Ashwell Street**, which crosses at the top.

 (4)

At an **Icknield Way** signpost, turn right along a shady path which borders a small factory on the left. It soon joins a stony lane at a marker post; keep ahead here, passing housing and allotments to reach a T-junction with an **Icknield Way** sign, opposite boarded-up **Partridge Hall**.

(For a SHORT CUT turn right.)

 (5)

Turn left and follow the wide track uphill, passing two cottages. Look for an opening in the hedge on the right where a signpost (**Arbury Banks Ancient Monument**) points across a field.

 (6)

Bear slightly left and make for the ugly farm fence ringing **Arbury Banks**. (The open views from the hill fort, which was in use from the late Bronze Age and throughout the Iron Age, emphasize its defensive position.) Bear left and then right, passing an unusual memorial inside the fence, to reach a farm track below a hedged bank or lynchet. Turn left along this to a copse. One path carries on ahead, but turn right, along a wide path which goes through the middle of fields.

 (7)

Cross **Newnham Road** (signpost) and continue along a wide permissive path (marker post) through fields. When the track meets a hedgerow, go through to a T-junction of paths. (Spread out below is a huge plain reaching into Bedfordshire and Cambridgeshire.) Turn right and walk downhill, passing gardens to meet **Hinxworth Road** (signpost). Turn right here for a short way to a road junction.

 (8)

Cross the road and turn left along the main road, avoiding the junction with Back Street.

*The brick wall on the left curves round a Victorian brewer's house. The former brewery office is next to the gateposts leading to the village hall, which is housed in an old maltings of Page's brewery. On the right is thatched 16th century **Chantry House**, which has a 15th century stone window at one end. Further on are the converted listed barns of **Farrows Farm**.*

*Cross **Wilson's Lane** and pass the low windows of **The Old Cottage**, one of the oldest houses in the village. Further on is early 16th century **Dixies Farmhouse**, now two dwellings. The barns (**Dixies Yard**) are now converted into businesses and houses. On the other side of the road is the ancient shop window of **The Old Saddlery** (17th century in*

Drive and Stroll

origin) looking over the street to **Bear House**, *a former farmhouse and inn built about 1480, on the corner of* **Bear Lane**. *On the opposite corner stands jettied* **Kirby Manor**. *On the corner of* **Bacon's Yard**, *stands 17th century* **Digswell Manor**, *which has an old malthouse chimney in its curving peg-tiled roof.*

Turn left into **Gardiner's Lane**, looking ahead for a glimpse of the listed thatched cob wall which is home to masonry bees, before turning right into **Swan Street** alongside the village-owned **Cottage Garden** to reach the **museum**, originally the tithe house for collecting rents for the Abbot of Westminster. The row of pretty white cottages opposite once housed the dreaded workhouse. **Swan House** – formerly The Angel in 1609, and later the Swan Inn – is on the corner.

Turn left down **Mill Street** passing the unusual 15th century double lychgate and the **Bushel and Strike** pub. Merchant Taylor's House built in 1681 has a historic plaque over its door. Walk over **Rollys Lane** and continue down **Mill Street**, passing pargetted cottages, the gateway to **The Bury** – which was restored by Lutyens and has a garden designed by Gertrude Jekyll – to the mill. Bear right round **Cow Lane**, ignoring the footpath to the left, and continue to the next road junction. Avoiding the left turn, keep ahead up **Springhead**. Pass pretty cottages to reach the **springs** basin, where a path goes through a kissing gate and leads across the source of the river Cam (information board) via stepping stones. Then go up steps and turn left to the road.

The less intrepid can walk up the lane, **Springhead**, and turn right along the springs' railings.

Places of Interest Nearby

Ashwell Village Museum is in a Tudor building with displays from the Stone Age onwards. Telephone: 01462 742956. The 14th century church of St Mary the Virgin has notable graffiti portraying old St Paul's Cathedral and haunting plague descriptions of 1350.